Contemporary Challenges in Securing Human Rights

edited by Corinne Lennox

D1341595

ISBN 978-0-9931102-2-1

Institute of Commonwealth Studies
School of Advanced Study
University of London
Senate House
Malet Street
London WC1E 7HU

Contents

Foreword

James Manor

In the early 1990s, all but one Master's degree programme on human rights in the world approached the topic from a narrowly legal perspective. They were mostly located in departments or schools of law. They had great virtues, as I had discovered when interacting with the programme at the Harvard Law School during the mid-1980s. But they largely omitted scholars from other disciplines – the social sciences, history, philosophy, etc. – who could offer crucial insights for a rounded understanding of human rights.

With this in mind, I began investigating the possibility of launching a multi-disciplinary Master's programme at the Institute of Commonwealth Studies in the University of London where I then taught. The sole exception to those law-based programmes was located not far away, at the University of Essex. But we had one major advantage over Essex. We had a rich array of human rights organisations on our doorstep, in London. Indeed, just one part of London – Islington – contains more headquarters for international rights organisations than does Vienna, Geneva, Paris or quite possibly New York.

That implied that a Master's degree programme in London could benefit enormously if practitioners from these organisations would share their rich experiences with students. So our setting argued not just for a multi-disciplinary approach to *understanding* human rights, but also for a degree programme that paid great attention to the problems and opportunities that arise for practitioners who focus on *securing* human rights. Out of this grew our MA programme in 'Understanding and Securing Human Rights'.

Our idea for such a programme received a warm welcome from Pierre Sané who then presided over the international headquarters of Amnesty International, which was within walking distance of the Institute. He agreed to provide practitioners, free of charge, to explain their work to students. In exchange, the Institute agreed to take on as students, free of charge, practitioners from Amnesty. Other human rights organisations in London – and certain organisations which engaged with rights as part of larger activities (such as the Trades Union Congress) – also agreed to send practitioners for seminars. This enabled us to mount a complete set of weekly seminars with practitioners throughout the academic year.

Several of these organisations were also willing to allow our students to do voluntary work as interns. Those arrangements started small since the numbers of students in the early years were rather limited, but they have blossomed mightily over the years as student numbers have expanded.

Some students, after completing their degrees, managed to find employment in these or other rights organisations. Others have obtained jobs in government agencies around the world, and in international organisations which deal with a broader range of issues, but for whom a background in human rights is highly relevant. At a dinner in Myanmar, in early 2015, I encountered a young woman from the staff of the United Nations Development Programme who offered perceptive assessments of changes in that country. When I asked where she had studied before joining UNDP and she replied that she had done the MA in Understanding and Securing Human Rights at the Institute.

It has attracted many able and committed students over the years. This was true from the start. During the MA's first year, we organised a party at the Institute in the depths of January, mainly as a morale booster amid the short days and the wretched weather. It was attended by Sir Robert Fellowes, a member of the Institute's board and the principal Secretary to the Queen. He was impressed by the idealism and intelligence of the students, and a few days later, they were invited to attend one of the summer garden parties at Buckingham Palace. That has become unworkable in more recent years as student numbers have risen, but the quality of the students has remained high.

I have often been asked why an Institute of *Commonwealth* Studies should have created an MA in human rights. This is actually not at all strange. Consider three things.

First, it was in the Institute that the Commonwealth Human Rights Initiative had been established, and when the MA got started, its main office was still within the walls (it later moved its headquarters to New Delhi).

Second, the Commonwealth, as an organisation, was then deepening its commitment to rights and to democratic politics. It was in that era that a Commonwealth Secretary-General led discussions at a Heads of Government Meeting in which the presidents of three member states with illiberal one-party regimes rose to announce, one after another, that they were relaxing constraints and adopting competitive multi-party systems.

Finally, the MA was established in the period when Nelson Mandela was elected President of South Africa. That carried especially potent meaning for the Institute. For decades, it had run a famous seminar series on southern Africa where leading scholars in the anti-apartheid movement exchanged insights on the way forward. Albie Sachs, a prominent figure in that movement and later a justice on the new South Africa's Constitutional Court, had been in residence – drawing together ideas that went into his country's new Constitution with its strong commitment to rights. And most startlingly, a safe in the Institute library had been the secret repository of Mandela's papers throughout his time in prison – including the text, in his hand, of his historic speech from the dock in Rivonia. Events in South Africa created a special sense of hope in the Institute which made it seem an appropriate place for an MA in human rights.

Hopes have dimmed somewhat since those days. In 2013, the Commonwealth betrayed its record as a force for human decency when it agreed to hold its Heads of Government Meeting in Sri Lanka which was then ruled by a squalid clique that was brazenly contemptuous of human rights – although voters there later shamed the Commonwealth by throwing the abusers out. In Britain, the Blair government eroded the freedoms of speech and of assembly, the right to a jury trial, and *habeus corpus*. It also sustained a change made by the Conservatives that undermined the right to silence by persons under police questioning, which brought the presumption of innocence into question. It did all of those things *before* 11 September 2001. Thereafter, excessive responses to terrorism by the Bush administration and others eroded rights still further. Several important countries have become increasingly contemptuous of rights: Hungary, Russia, Egypt, Turkey, Pakistan, and most of Southeast and Central Asia. China has intensified its assault on rights, and its baleful influence is felt across much of the developing world – not least in Africa.

As the challenges have grown, so has the need for the kind of work that is done in the MA programme – and latterly, in the Human Rights Consortium that grew out of it. This book celebrates the work in recent years, but more importantly, it demonstrates a firm resolve to persist.

1

Introduction

Corinne Lennox

It has been a great pleasure to put together this edited volume to commemorate the first 20 years of the MA in Understanding and Securing Human Rights. In doing so, I have been able to reach back to the earliest days of the programme to learn how it developed in close cooperation with staff at Amnesty International and other human rights NGOs. Surprisingly, the programme of three core modules, namely 'Understanding Human Rights', 'Securing Human Rights' and 'Translating Human Rights into Law' have constituted the structure of the MA since its inception. It was thus appropriate to choose these three pillars as the framing themes of the book.

I was also keen to highlight the achievements of the graduates across time, space and field of specialisation. I'm pleased that we have been able to feature the work of alumni in varied aspects of human rights, from classic civil and political rights like the right to a fair trial (Shah), to the use of poetry for human rights (Sumpton), the protection of the environment (Venisnik), the burgeoning field of business and human rights (Dhanarajan) and human rights in the digital age (Marcus). The authors were invited to submit 'think pieces' drawing from their own work, both academic and practitioner-based, and using the skills developed on the MA. It is a credit to the programme that the chapters are rich with critical analysis, legal expertise and innovative approaches.

Understanding human rights

The book begins with a set of essays that help us in 'Understanding Human Rights' by considering the construction of rights from a social and political perspective. Short opens with a brief history of how two key disciplines, Sociology and Anthropology, came to offer insightful and often critical examinations of the evolving human rights regime. In particular, these disciplines show us that rights are contextual and socially formed. In Barreto's chapter, we take one step back to think about why scholars have sought to elaborate a theory of human rights in the first place. He posits several possible motivations but comes to rest on the argument that human rights theory is solidarity, which resonates nicely with Short's review of the 'activist' strand of social science scholarship.

Ojulari offers an excellent illustration of this social constructionist perspective. She examines the case of the emerging rights corpus for people of African descent in Colombia, drawing from critical race theory to show how the domestic laws promulgated have been more constraining for Afro-Colombians than emancipatory. This is a helpful reminder that we cannot understand human rights laws at face value: instead, we must ask, in whose interests do these rights operate? Souter's chapter takes a similar tack in his examination of the concept of the 'responsibility to protect' (R2P). He argues that the norm has been too narrowly interpreted, usually in the interests of states, but also reflected in the limited understandings of R2P articulated by advocates. He encourages advocates to push the normative boundaries of human rights concepts in his focus on reparation rights for refugees in host countries. The final chapter in this section also looks at fast-moving normative boundaries, bringing us into the 'digital age' of human rights. Marcus summarises some of the many implications that changes in information and communication technologies can and are having for existing human rights or for creating new rights.

These chapters demonstrate that we can expand concepts of rights beyond the often narrow and restrictive policy interpretations that are currently hegemonic. Moreover, rights need to respond to changes in social reality. Indeed, if they do not so respond, they risk becoming moribund. We all have a role to play in shaping new 'understandings' of human rights.

Securing human rights

This leads nicely to the second section of the book, 'Securing Human Rights'. I currently teach this module and have had the privilege to listen to the reflections, advice and frustrations of many practitioners over the years. I like to remind students that the information conveyed in those sessions is like 'gold dust' – extremely valuable to gather when practitioners have a brief moment to share it. In this way, the MA classroom has thus served also as a small oasis for our guest lecturers, who have the opportunity in constructing their lectures and in responding to student questions to reflect on the implicit strategies in their daily work.

We begin this section with a new and emerging tool for activists to do this reflection more systematically as a key stage of the programme planning cycle: 'theories of change'. Theories of change demand a much more critical and nuanced consideration of our own assumptions of how to secure human rights. Gready's chapter usefully contrasts the theories of change prevalent in the work of human rights actors and development actors. In doing so he underscores some broad differences in approach that help to explain why state actors have often been more receptive to development practitioners than human rights advocates. These points are taken up by Klirodotakou in her chapter on support to women's human rights. She discusses how development funding is being channelled to women as change agents, without full consideration of the most effective process of change needed. Support has moved away from grassroots women's movements towards top-down approaches, despite contrary evidence that change is more likely through women's empowerment and mobilisation at a local level. Holt's chapter on conflict prevention shows how a human rights 'informed' approach can be more instrumentally valuable in situations of inter-cultural conflict than strict advocacy on international human rights law. The theories of change implicit in human rights may not always be appropriate for conflict transformation and prevention, particularly where the norms *per se* are resisted by local actors.

Other chapters in this section look at new avenues for securing human rights. Burrows discusses her work in the tax justice campaigns of ActionAid. Tax has been a too-long neglected dimension of human rights advocacy, perhaps because of blinkered understandings of financing for human rights. Dhanarajan dives into the business and human rights field, where non-treaty based systems of regulation are proliferating. This raises the important question of whether non-legally binding regimes can be more effective than law in securing human rights. Hamdan considers the role of Technical Cooperation Programmes (TCPs) delivered by the UN at the invitation of states. TCPs are considered the softer approach to norm compliance for UN agencies and his examples from Saudi Arabia show that advancements can be made through socialisation processes such as training, network construction and dialogue. Sumpton describes how poetry can be a powerful tool for securing human rights, both in transforming meanings of rights but also in empowering rights holders through new forms of self-expression and recovery from human rights violations.

Translating human rights into law

Finally, the third section of the book brings us to reflections on 'Translating Human Rights into Law'. Shah opens this section with her chapter on cuts to legal aid in the UK and the far-reaching effects. This reminds us that access to justice is contingent on a number of factors even in countries with an otherwise strong rule of law. Ball extends this discussion with her chapter on the experience of supporting cases from Australia to the UN treaty body system. Among her key points is the important role that NGOs can play in enabling cases to be heard, echoing Shah's discussion on UK civil society support to those newly excluded from legal aid.

The following chapters from Cantor and Sait examine the role of human rights law when intersecting with other legal regimes. Cantor offers some suggestions on how international human rights law could complement refugee law in situations of extra-territorial protection of refugees. Sait shares insights from his study on property rights for women under Islamic law, rights which he argues are instrumental for the realisation of other human rights for women. He shows the contribution that rights-based approaches can make to transforming meanings within cultural and customary legal systems.

This collection of essays is also an important reminder of the limitations of the law used in isolation from other strategies of advocacy. Litigation and legislation are just one component of socialisation and persuasion in achieving changes in behaviour of states (or increasingly non-state actors). Engstrom's chapter on the Inter-American Human Rights System illustrates the political and social dimensions that impact on the strength of that regime. On litigation in the Inter-American system, he argues that it has not always served the direct interests of the applicants, being used often instead for wider legislative and policy aims that may neglect more specific remedies for individuals. Venisnik makes a related plea in her chapter to ensure that litigation achieves 'power to the people' rather than being a strategy imposed by outsiders. Nevertheless, her case studies from Southeast Asia show that litigation in various guises can have a useful impact for communities. Waiti illustrates the value of the Universal Periodic Review (UPR) for achieving legislation and policy change. He describes the promulgation of the UN Convention on the Rights of Persons with Disabilities into national law in the Marshall Islands following UPR recommendations. This processes was important not only for legal change but also for building civil society and for socialisation on disability rights.

Conclusion

I hope this edited book serves as a useful legacy of the MA in Understanding and Securing Human Rights. We are pleased to be able to offer it also as an open access online resource via the School of Advanced Study. I would like to take this opportunity to thank the contributors for producing excellent chapters under a tight time frame and whilst juggling their difficult day-jobs. I would also like to thank the current MA students who have assisted in the editing of the book and the organisation of the MA 20th anniversary conference, including Genna, Danni, Chucks, Justine, Emily, Ana, Christian, Megan, Minah, Joe, Iyanu and Anabel.

There are more than 700 alumni of this programme working around the globe towards the full implementation of human rights for all in very different ways. They each have a unique story to tell of what brought them to the study of human rights in the first place. A few have shared those stories here. I hope that in doing so they will help to inspire future students of human rights.

Part 1

Understanding Human Rights

2

Researching and studying human rights: interdisciplinary insight

Damien Short

Since 1948, the study of human rights has been dominated by legal scholarship that has sought to investigate the development of human rights law, emerging jurisprudence, regional systems, the decisions and recommendations of human rights mechanisms and institutions and to a lesser extent the 'compliance gaps' between state commitments and actions. Even so, in all of these spheres there are elements that cannot be fully understood through a purely legal lens, moreover, if we understand 'human rights' more broadly, and look into the practical world of human rights work and human rights discourse, advocacy and activism, then we need to go beyond legal analysis. Indeed, to understand the world of human rights in both theory and practice requires interdisciplinary insight, as it covers an enormous range of social, political, economic and environmental issues. In this chapter, I will outline the contributions of two disciplines that were slow to contribute to the field of human rights but which offer vitally important insights that can guide both academic research and human rights advocacy.

Sociological insights

Sociology was initially sceptical with the normativity that is attached to human rights along with the claim of universality, which saw a sociology of citizenship effectively act as a substitute for a sociology of human rights. In a series of seminal contributions in the 1990s, Bryan Turner argued that the concept of citizenship, however, is closely linked with the modern nation state, a political form that has been infected with the problems of imperialism, globalisation, migrant workers, refugees, and Indigenous peoples (Short 2009). In a key essay for the journal *Sociology*, Turner (1993) suggested that globalisation has created problems that are not wholly internal to nation states and that consequently we should extend sociological inquiry to the concept of *human* rights. While few sociologists have attempted (like Turner) to develop a foundational social theory of human rights, there is now a growing body of research that embraces a more social constructionist view of human rights.

From a social constructionist perspective *universal* human rights should be seen as 'historically and socially contingent, the product of a particular time, place, and set of circumstances, and a work in permanent progress' (Morris 2006, 26). A sociological approach to rights discourses, practices, and struggles is necessary to identify the mechanisms that translate social phenomena into rights disputes. Yet, viewing rights this way suggests that we must pay due attention to the social actors involved in their invention/construction if we are to understand rights regimes fully.

Within this broad social constructionist sociology we can see an important dimension of sociological enquiry begin to emerge, i.e. the role of *power* in the domain of human rights. Human rights scholar Michael Freeman (2002), in a major interdisciplinary contribution to the area, identifies rights *institutionalisation* as a social process and he also displays an acute awareness of the role of power in that process, which he sees as perhaps the major sociological contribution. He writes:

> The institutionalisation of human rights may ... lead, not to their more secure protection, but to their protection in a form that is less threatening to the existing system of power. The *sociological* point is not that human rights should never be institutionalised, but, rather, that institutionalisation is a social process, involving power, and that it should be analysed and not assumed to be beneficial (Freeman 2002, 85).

Freeman further argues that the social sciences have been 'excessively legalistic' and overemphasised the UN system whilst neglecting to look deeper into the role of powerful global institutions and global power politics, most notably the G7, the Bretton Woods institutions, and the foreign policy of the US, in both the violation and construction of human rights (Freeman 2002, 177). The discipline of sociology is well placed to investigate the role of *power* in this regard.

Social research has shown how rights should be viewed as instrumentally useful strategic resources invoked by social actors in competition for power in domestic and international arenas (Short 2009). Rights can be constructed through the interplay of domestic and international forces and will be reinforced as long as otherwise powerless social actors find no other alternative but to engage in rights talk. Sociology may be the discipline best equipped to discuss the social forces that underline the genesis of such rights and the social struggles from which they materialise (Short 2009). A primary task for sociologists is to become intimately familiar with the advocates, their claims, and the social processes through which rights are constructed, while being careful to balance claims for universal applicability with the empirical reality of social and cultural diversity in the world. Sociological researchers are also well placed to examine the 'considerable gap between the recognition of the need for protection and its achievements in practice' (Morris 2006, 3). Sociological researchers should ask some very important questions such as: How are rights socially constructed—by whom, for whom, and in what social context? How and why do particular social actors and groups claim and access rights? How are rights affected by the social, political, and economic context in which they emerge and operate? What role is played by social structures—are they enabling, constraining, or both? To what extent are rights guaranteed or limited by the law? Have power relations affected the construction and functionality of rights? Whose interests do rights actually work to protect?

In summary, the discipline of sociology is well equipped to expose, discuss, and possibly amend obvious limitations in existing conceptions of rights, especially the formal legalistic dimensions, the limitations of which, as we shall see later, are something that social anthropologist Richard Wilson is also concerned to 'move beyond' (1997). Such sociological research is now gathering pace. Indeed, the British Sociological Association now has a 'Sociology of Rights' study group, from which has already emerged a major contribution to the subfield entitled 'Sociology and Human Rights: New Engagements' (Hynes, Lamb, Short, and Waites 2011).

Anthropological insights

The issue of cultural relativism has of course influenced both sociological and anthropological perspectives on human rights. It was a major factor that led sociology to take such a long time to engage with the phenomena at all; while anthropology, on the other hand, was an influential voice at the outset of the international codification of human rights norms (Short 2009, 97).

The discipline of anthropology has evolved to be concerned with the study of the entire range of cultures and societies in the world. Given such scope, there are significant points of convergence between anthropology and sociology. Yet in the early stages of its development the discipline tended to focus on non-Western 'primitive' societies, which led to important differences between the disciplines (Short 2009, 97). Sociology historically tended to focus on Western societies, which thus generated methodological and theoretical differences between the two disciplines. For example, when Western sociologists studied their own society they could take much context for granted before hypothesising about their data, while anthropologists studying other cultures could make few safe assumptions and consequently developed an holistic methodology that emphasised that each social entity or group has its own identity that is *distinct* and not reducible to individual constituent parts. Consequently, anthropology would not assume that all cultures shared the same values, which is the fundamental ontological position that guided the discipline's early attitude towards the notion of universal human rights.

Consequently a key school of thought for those anthropologists seeking to engage with the world of human rights sought to use the discipline's ethnographic methodology to explore and investigate the 'social practice of human rights' or, as Richard Wilson puts it, 'the social life of rights' (1997). Wilson, a social anthropologist, agrees with the main thrust of the sociological approaches that were discussed above, arguing that social scientists should be primarily concerned with analysing rights as socially constructed phenomena. He writes:

> The intellectual efforts of those seeking to develop a framework for understanding the social life of rights would be better directed not towards foreclosing their ontological status, but instead by exploring their meaning and use. What is needed are more detailed studies of human rights according to the actions and intentions of social actors, within wider historical constraints of institutionalised power. (Wilson 1997, 3–4)

Taking up this call, researchers began to focus on an increase in negotiations and claims made by various social groups *in a language of 'rights'*. A trend began to emerge in which long-established theoretical debates about concepts such as rights, justice, and citizenship began to engage with empirical 'data' that contextualises rights-claiming processes (Short 2009). Anthropologists started to advocate the need to explore how exactly universal concepts were being used in local struggles. In essence, the relationship between culture and rights was seen as an issue to be studied *empirically*. The thrust of this approach is thus descriptive and makes no claim to endorse the universality of human rights. It is an effort to uncover how human rights actually function in an empirical sense, to uncover what they mean to different social actors in different social contexts. More attention was gradually being paid to empirical, contextual analyses of specific rights struggles. This intellectual strategy sought to record how individuals, groups, communities, and states use rights discourse in the pursuit of particular ends, and how they become enmeshed in its logic (Short 2009, 98).

Anthropology's relativistic perspective was borne out of a detached scientific methodology that frequently observed a plethora of value systems in its research 'subjects'. This 'detached' approach, however, did not last as the dominant perspective. While many anthropologists were able to maintain an 'objective' detachment from their research subjects, increasingly this approach gave way to immersion and empathy, which in turn led to political activism on behalf of the subjects.

Those who advocated such an approach argued that anthropological understandings of specific cultural processes, which are embedded in wider (what sociologists would term 'structural') social power relationships, should be used to bolster specific endeavours for social change and/or to assist specific marginalised peoples, populations, or groups in resisting threats to their survival (Short 2009). This approach views human rights as a useful tool for serving an ethical commitment towards threatened peoples and cultures. The effectiveness of human rights as a tool in this sense can be greatly improved through more expansive and inclusive definitions. Thus, there is a normative suggestion within this approach that anthropologists *should* work to expand the definitions of *human rights* so as to increase their effectiveness for marginalised groups and cultures—an approach termed 'emancipatory cultural politics' (Short 2009, 98). This approach, which encourages anthropological engagement with human rights discourse as a political strategy for the protection of threatened populations, was perhaps the first major disciplinary current to emerge in the anthropology of human rights. Perhaps the most notable recent research within this broad approach is that of Shannon Speed, which she has termed 'critically engaged activist research' (Speed 2006, 66). This approach is concerned to embrace the issues raised by the social actors, not shy away from engagement and commentary, and in fact warns against an *overly detached* anthropology of human rights (Speed 2006, 66). The focus of the research is not just about *research on* human rights in the particular site—Chiapas, Mexico—but also *advocacy for* human rights there. Consequently, it could be suggested that such research does not fall into the trap of forgetting the 'human' in human rights. For the social actors suffering injustice, human rights are much more than an academic curiosity (Short 2009).

Conclusion

We have seen how from an initial position of scepticism there is now a growing body of research emerging from both sociology and anthropology that seeks to explore the construction, meaning, use and functioning of rights, and for some, the secondary goal is to use this data to work for the protection of human rights through critically engaged activist research. It is this latter approach which has informed all of my teaching on the MA Understanding and Securing Human Rights at the Institute of Commonwealth Studies. Furthermore, in addition to the knowledge gleaned from legal, philosophical, and political approaches to the study of human rights, when I teach our Understanding Human Rights module, I strongly urge students to embrace interdisciplinary and, in particular, anthropological and sociological studies that explore the 'social life of rights', since it is only through such studies that we can hope to understand fully the *practice* of human rights in the modern world.

Bibliography

Freeman, M. (2002) *Human Rights: An Interdisciplinary Approach* (Malden, MA: Polity).

Hynes, P., M. Lamb, D. Short and M. Waites (2011) *Sociology and Human Rights: New Engagements* (London: Routledge).

Morris, L. (ed.) (2006) *Rights: Sociological Perspectives* (Abingdon: Routledge).

Short, D. (2009) 'Sociological and Anthropological Approaches', in M. Goodhart (ed.), *Human Rights Politics and Practice* (Oxford: Oxford University Press), chapter 6.

Speed, S. (2006) 'At the crossroads of human rights and anthropology: toward a critically engaged activist research', *American Anthropologist* 108 (1), pp. 66–76.

Turner, B. S. (2006) *Vulnerability and Human Rights* (University Park, PA: The Pennsylvania State University Press).

Wilson, R. (1997) 'Human rights, culture and context: an introduction', in R. Wilson (ed.), *Human Rights, Culture and Context: Anthropological Perspectives* (London: Pluto Press), pp. 1–27.

3

Human rights theory as solidarity

José-Manuel Barreto

> *'The state of mind is that of*
> *passionate sympathetic contemplation (θεωρία),*
> *in which the spectator is identified with the suffering God,*
> *dies in his death, and rises again in his new birth'*
> F.M. Cornford,
> on the meaning of the word *theory* in the Dionysian cult

> *'I have had no other interest but this:*
> *to liberate [the Indians] from the violent deaths*
> *which they have suffered and suffer...*
> *through compassion at seeing multitudes of people*
> *who are rational'*
> Bartolomé de las Casas, in his will

Let's formulate some questions that are important for those who are engaged in making theory of human rights but which are rarely thematised: Why do legal theory? Why are scholars interested in elaborating a theory of human rights? A number of answers come to the tip of the tongue: in order justify and advance the cause of human rights; as a way of fulfilling political or ideological commitments; as a result of a commitment to justice or to the enforcement of rule of law; to learn about the phenomenon of the law; because it is part of the business of the academy; out of a professional duty and as a way of earning a living; due to the pleasure of fiddling with theories and abstract thinking. It can also be the consequence of the combination of some or all the above motives.

Above all, let's try a different track to answer these questions. Baxi has complained about how recent and sophisticated Western theories of democracy and human rights ignore the materiality of the violation of human rights or the voices of those who suffer, in a well-established feature of academic common sense that he describes as the 'cruelty of theory' (2002, 14). In a similar way, Horkheimer's critique of Kantian morality did not only attack the metaphysical way of thinking but it also pointed to the theorists themselves. Horkheimer did not criticise the metaphysical 'forgetting of being' as Heidegger did, but the immoral character of the forgetfulness of the suffering of the wretched of the earth and their struggles in history (Brunkhorst 1993, 78). For Horkheimer, metaphysicians and theorists are scarcely 'impressed by what torments humanity' and, while their reflections on history and society are irreproachably 'objective', 'suffering or even outrage over justice, or sympathy with victims' are foreign to them (Schmitt 1993, 29).

This inability to look at those who suffer and the retreat of philosophy, critical legal theory and human rights theory 'from the scenes of the battlefield' has to do with their immersion in the intellectual modern culture. A theory indifferent to suffering and obsessed with objectivity or justification is just the expression of the platonic and modern conception of philosophy as theory of knowledge or epistemology. In modernity, to think philosophically supposes a search for objectivity for the conditions that must be present to ensure knowledge can aspire to truth. The question confronting the philosophical effort is that of how the subject can get access to the object in such a way that ideas or concepts attained during this process apprehend the object as it is. This was the hegemonic form that philosophy adopted from the historical dawn of modernity. Having its remote antecedents in Plato, philosophy as epistemology acquired a dominant position with the emergence of transcendental subjectivism. Philosophy dwelled and remained imprisoned within the vicious circle of the relationship between subject and object, which constitutes the plane inhabited by the doubts of Descartes' cogito that aspires to certitude. It is in this realm that the subject takes distance from the empirical world and from common sense and advances towards the transcendental pure *a priori*, as in Kant. This is also the case of the sphere in which Hegel's dialectic between subject and object occurs and leads to absolute knowledge.

Later, in the context of the 20th century Anglo-North American philosophical tradition, a survey of the ways in which philosophy developed under the Neo-Kantian hegemony shows philosophy as consisting basically of conceptual analysis, explication of meaning, examination of the logic of language and of the structure of the activity of mind (Rorty 1979, 12). In all of these forms of philosophical work, it is also the question of truth and meaning that drives the task of thinking. Thus, the way of thinking inaugurated by the Socrates-Plato partnership, re-launched by Descartes and pursued by Neokantian analytical philosophy, marks modern philosophy with its epistemological character (Rorty 1979, 156–64).

In the human rights arena the epistemological ethos of modern philosophy turns, as in Kant, into a sustained reflection on human dignity, which is deduced from the universal maxims that rule human conduct, namely the different instantiations of the categorical imperative. Turning from anthropology to pure reason, ethical norms are reached by a process in which moral reason takes distance from any empirical experience. This 'metaphysics of morals' guarantees the construction of *a priori* laws, which are necessary and universal and therefore are to be obeyed by all (Kant 1978, 5–6). In one of its formulations, the imperative of pure practical reason prescribes that human beings should never be treated as means alone but also as ends. The consequence derived from the categorical imperative is the principle according to which being human is to be understood as an end-in-itself. This principle sustains the dignity of all human beings that, in turn, becomes the foundation of human rights. The epistemological orientation of modern philosophy has also led the tradition to conceive of the theory of rights as conceptual analysis, in order to make the concept of human rights clear and to define their meaning (Freeman 2002, 2). It also points to an engagement with 'the truth of human rights', namely with a reflection on topics such as the characterisation of human nature, the 'existence' itself of human rights and the definition of what precisely they are (Donnelly 1985, 1).

Rorty believes that the task of thinking should rest on our relations with other human beings and should not be constructed 'in terms of our relation to non-human reality' (1985, 25). Platonism and Kantianism have weakened the ability of our culture to 'listen to outsiders' and to be sensitive to those 'who are suffering' (Rorty 1991a, 13). A philosophy overwhelmingly concerned with truth and epistemological subjectivism distracts or distances us from our fellow human beings and blurs our sense of solidarity (Rorty 1999, xv). This is due to the fact that our readiness to note and to become involved with those subjected to pain and humiliation is not cultivated or simply neglected. When philosophy consists basically of a reiterative formulation of metaphysical or epistemological questions, it is natural to forget or to relegate human and social suffering as secondary matters, assuming that they are just appearances or the product of a common sense way of looking at the world (Rorty 1996a, 74). In this intellectual climate suffering becomes an odd topic or even a non-philosophical theme.

Rorty's critique of Platonic and Kantian epistemological philosophy supposes a prioritisation of ethics over theory of knowledge, and the inclusion of the quest for knowledge within the ethical endeavour. In a move that resembles Levinas' priority of ethics over ontology, Rorty asserts a precedence of ethics over epistemology: knowledge is basically orientated by an ethical and political interest in solidarity (1991b, 24; 27). The specifically epistemological duties of a philosophy as solidarity are those of putting together and generalising our intuitions, always with a practical aim, which in some cases could be that of how strengthening the self-awareness, power and efficacy of human rights culture (Rorty 1994, 117).

Rorty attempts, as Dewey did before, a critique of the vision of philosophy as theory of knowledge out of a longing for less cruel and less unjust societies (1979, 13). Anti-foundationalism is, in this sense, a move from philosophy

[handwritten top margin: Critical Theory = philosophical approach to culture, esp literature that considers social, historical & ideological forces & structures which produce & constrain it]

understood as epistemology to philosophy understood as solidarity. In this framework, objectivity is not the goal of inquiry but the alleviation of the pain others are enduring. The force driving the intellectual adventure is not that of a quest for truth, a love for knowledge, a will to know or a 'desire for an epistemology' (Rorty 1979, 163). Rather, it is an impulse or 'desire for solidarity' (Rorty 1991, 21), for answering the plea of fellow human beings. Our impulse to think and the spontaneous inclination to do philosophy or legal theory come from our 'openness to strangers', from a concern, a preoccupation or an intuitive apprehension for those who are victims of violence. That openness allows us to be witness to the suffering of others and to cultivate inside us a fellow feeling (Rorty 1979, 9). In this perspective the pursuit of freedom, solidarity, and human rights and the struggle against oppression, humiliation and cruelty are the forces driving philosophical inquiry (Rorty 1989, xiii).

The ethics of sympathy developed within the ambit of Critical Theory can also be drawn into this discussion on the nature of theory. If the basic interest of Critical Theory is, according to Horkheimer, that of 'striving to reduce suffering' (McCarthy 1993, 138), theory acquires an ethical drive and takes the form of an 'existential judgement' (Brunkhorst 1993, 72). It is said that Adorno was also close to this impulse, as sympathy with the suffering of the victims of violence acted as motivation of his thinking (Morchen, cited in Garcia-Duttmann 2002, 6). If the experience of individual suffering is at the basis of social criticism (McCole 1993, 18), then the main object of theory is not the search for truth but rather the practical aim of the alleviation of pain. But again, such an object is not defined in abstract or rationalistic terms: the relief of the suffering — which is human, both individual and social, and that of past, present and future generations — becomes the teleology of morality and theory, and the political motive of the critical theorist.

[handwritten left margin: evidence of design in nature]

The idea of philosophy as solidarity has, as a consequence, a partisan conception of philosophy. In an epistemologically orientated theory the subject is in front of the object — society or the world — and just in front of it, being in this way a spectator. To step outside or to remain at a distance from the society with which we are dealing is assumed to be a necessary condition for objective knowledge. This would allow the analysis of a particular society from a universal or transcendental point of view. This does not occur in a philosophy built out of a feeling of sympathy or solidarity. In this scenario, the one who knows is a participant who reflects upon the situation and acts upon it (Rorty 1979, 18–19). Those developing theory are engaged in a relation with those under scrutiny, occupied in learning how to deal with the situation in which others are involved, and eager to make a contribution to that community. Theory is conceived of as 'cooperative human inquiry' and the Neopragmatist philosopher is seen as a 'partisan of solidarity' (Rorty 1991, 21; 24) — as somebody who serves the community (Rorty 1996b, 17).

The implications of such a conception of philosophy are present in Rorty's theory of human rights. *Human Rights, Rationality and Sentimentality*, Rorty's only piece entirely dedicated to reflect on human rights, begins with the image of a Muslim man being physically and psychologically destroyed on the orders of his Serbs captors in Bosnia. This text later develops into a meditation about long term cultural strategies that ensure this kind of atrocities do not happen again. In a more traditional tone, Michael Freeman's *Human Rights* begins with a story about the fate of a Pakistani teenager who is raped, handed by the police to her family and finally murdered as a punishment for dishonouring her tribe. Maintaining that 'the analysis of the concept of human rights... must be combined with a sympathetic understanding of the human experiences to which the concept refers', and assuming that 'we sympathise with the victims', Freeman goes on to develop his chapter on *Thinking about Human Rights* (2002, 2–3). In a similar sense Costas Douzinas describes his *The End of Human Rights* as 'a critique of legal humanism inspired by a love of humanity' (2000, vii). The rhetorical devices used here to begin the analysis give us a clue about the origins or the compulsion that leads the theorist to think about human rights in the first place.

Rorty's Neopragmatism ends up as being a 'philosophy of solidarity' as hope, freedom and human rights substitute knowledge, truth or objectivity as guides of thinking (1991, 33). Theory is not created by a love of knowledge. It is openness to others and a desire for solidarity that makes us to think of rights. The theory of human rights is developed by theorists witnessing the pain of others and out of a desire to reduce their suffering. The human rights scholar wants to get involved and to intervene, and to take the side of the victim — of all victims — against all perpetrators. To be in front of those who are victims of cruelty, humiliation and oppression, and to look at the face of those who suffer are the experiences that give birth to the theory of human rights. Theories in general and legal theory in particular are consequences of sympathy. Human rights theory is solidarity.

Bibliography

Baxi, U. (2002) *The Future of Human Rights* (Delhi & Oxford: Oxford University Press).

Brunkhorst, H. (1993) 'Dialectical positivism of happiness: Horkheimer's materialist deconstruction of philosophy', in S. Benhabib et al. (eds.), *On Max Horkheimer. New Perspectives* (Cambridge, MA & London: MIT Press).

Donnelly, J. (1985) *The Concept of Human Rights* (London: Croom Helm).

Douzinas, C. (2000) *The End of Human Rights* (Oxford: Hart).

Freeman, M. (2002) *Human Rights: An Interdisciplinary Approach* (Malden, MA: Polity).

Garcia-Duttmann, A. (2002) *The Memory of Thought. An Essay on Heidegger and Adorno* (London & New York: Continuum).

Kant, I. (1978) *Foundations of the Metaphysics of Morals* (Indianapolis, IN: Bobbs-Merrill).

McCarthy, T. (1993) 'The idea of a critical theory and its relation to philosophy', in S. Benhabib et al. (eds.), *On Max Horkheimer. New Perspectives* (Cambridge, MA & London: MIT Press).

McCole, J. *et al.* (1993) 'Max Horkheimer: between philosophy and social science', in S. Benhabib et al. (eds.), *On Max Horkheimer. New Perspectives* (Cambridge, MA & London: MIT Press).

Rorty, R. (1979) *Philosophy and the Mirror of Nature* (Princeton, PA: Princeton University Press).

Rorty, R. (1989) *Contingency, Irony and Solidarity* (Cambridge: Cambridge University Press).

Rorty, R. (1991a) 'Introduction', in R. Rorty, *Objectivity, Relativism and Truth. Philosophical Papers I* (Cambridge: Cambridge University Press)

Rorty, R. (1991b) 'Solidarity or objectivity', in R. Rorty, *Objectivity, Relativism and Truth. Philosophical Papers I* (Cambridge: Cambridge University Press).

Rorty, R. (1994) 'Human rights, rationality and sentimentality', in S. Shute and S. Hurley (eds.), *On Human Rights: The Oxford Amnesty Lectures 1993* (New York: Basic Books).

Rorty, R. (1996a) 'Heidegger, Kundera and Dickens', in R. Rorty, *Essays on Heidegger and Others. Philosophical Papers. Volume 2* (Cambridge & New York: Cambridge University Press).

Rorty, R. (1996b) 'Philosophy as science, as metaphor and as politics', in R. Rorty *Essays on Heidegger and Others. Philosophical Papers. Volume 2* (Cambridge & New York: Cambridge University Press).

Rorty, R. (1999) *Philosophy and Social Hope* (London: Penguin).

Rorty, R. (2000) 'Universality and truth', in R. Brandom (ed.), *Rorty and his Critics* (Abingdon: Blackwell).

Schmitt, A. (1993) 'Max Horkheimer's intellectual physiognomy', in S. Benhabib et al. (eds.), *On Max Horkheimer. New Perspectives* (Cambridge, MA & London: MIT Press).

4

The social construction of Afro-descendant rights in Colombia

Esther Ojulari

Afro-descendant people make up around 30 per cent of the population of Latin America and the Caribbean, some 150 million people (IACHR 2011). In a context of *mestizaje* and the myth of racial democracy, Afro-descendant rights were not institutionalised in many Latin American states until the end of the 20th century. This reflected an invisibility at the international level where a specific normative framework on Afro-descendant rights did not begin to emerge until the beginning of the 21st century. Through multicultural citizenship reforms in the 1980s and 1990s several Latin American states recognised rights for their Afro-descendant populations; however, these tended to be subsumed into the existing indigenous rights framework, thus neglecting the specific situations of Afro-descendants.

Using theoretical concepts from the sociology of human rights and critical race theory (CRT) this chapter poses some key issues for analysing the institutionalisation of Afro-descendant rights in Latin America and, in particular, in Colombia. It draws on literature from the social constructionist perspective on human rights, which demonstrates how rights emerge in particular historical and political contexts and are institutionalised through processes of negotiation between states and civil society, often influenced by powerful economic and political interests (see Waters 1996; Freeman 2002; Morris 2006; Samson and Short 2006; Short 2007; Miller 2010; Haynes et al. 2011).

Critical race theory (CRT) places the issues of race and racism at the centre of analyses. With roots in critical legal studies, CRT critiqued US civil rights laws for failing to lead to significant change and rather serving the wider political and international interests of the State and white elite (see Bell 1995; Ladson-Billings and Tate IV 1995; Ladson-Billings 1998; Taylor et al, 2009; Delgado and Stefancic 2012). The chapter combines social constructionist theories with CRT concepts of structural racism, 'interest convergence' and 'model minorities' to explore the discourses, interests and processes which influenced the institutionalisation of Afro-descendant rights in Colombia.

Afro-descendant rights in context

Historic context: invisibilising racism

CRT views racism as structural, institutional and endemic to society in the United States (US), underpinning and informing all social relations (Taylor 2009; Delgado and Stefancic 2012). As part of post-independence, nation-building projects, many countries in Latin America promoted *mestizo* national identities that supposedly celebrated the racial and ethnic diversity of the nations (Andrews 2004). States espoused an idea of 'racial democracy' asserting that, in contrast to the Jim Crow segregation laws of the US, Latin American societies were characterised by harmonious race relations and racial equality (Gates Jr. 2012; Telles 2004; Cottrol 2001). However, the ideology of *mestizaje* has served to assimilate Afro-descendants and indigenous peoples denying their histories, cultures and contributions to their nations (de Friedman and Arocha 1995). Rather than removing racial categories, the ideology of *mestizaje* actually reconstructs categories re-establishing a basis for racism (Wade 2004). Both *mestizaje* and the myth of racial democracy were extremely influential in shaping racial discourse throughout the region, denying the existence of racism and creating barriers for Afro-descendant movements to make claims for racial justice (Safa 1998; Htun 2004; Reichmann 1999; Ng'weno 2012; Morrison 2012).

It has since been argued that racial democracy is a 'myth' as racism and racial inequality are very real problems throughout Latin America (Alberti and Araujo 2006). A wealth of literature shows that Afro-descendants are disproportionately represented among the most marginalised groups in the region and while often equated to class, the socio-economic inequalities they face are underpinned by structural discrimination and racism (Hasenbalg 1996; Safa 1998; Sanchez and Bryan 2003; Htun 2004; Murillo 2011; Inter-American Commission on Human Rights 2011; Leighton 2012; UNDP 2012; Telles 2014).

Political context – a space for model minorities?

The CRT concepts of 'model minorities' and 'differential racialisation' explore the ways in which different minority groups are racialised by mainstream society. For example, the stereotyping of certain minority groups in the US as 'successful' in education and employment based on hard work, often downplays experiences of racism and exclusion and is used to legitimise the low achievement and inequality of other groups, blaming them for their own lack of success (Delgado and Stefancic, 2012).

In Latin America, outside of the Brazilian context, the ideology of *mestizaje* was based on a binary between white European and indigenous peoples, promoting romantic celebration of an indigenous past, while excluding Afro-descendants (Paschel 2010; Wade 1997). This 'indigenous inclusion, black exclusion' (Hooker 2005) translated to a lack of policies and legislation recognising the existence and rights of Afro-descendants.

Towards the end of the 20th century, as indigenous rights were institutionalised at the international level, many countries in Latin America underwent multicultural citizenship reforms adopting new constitutions which recognised, the multicultural nature of their societies. Reflecting the language of ILO Convention 169 concerning Indigenous and Tribal Peoples in Independent Countries (1989), they included rights to territory, culture, language, identity, political participation and education for ethnic groups (Sieder 1998).

This ethnic rights discourse, however, provided limited space for inclusion of Afro-descendants, who had traditionally been imagined along racial rather than cultural/ethnic lines (Wade 1997). Only some of the States that adopted new constitutions included rights for their Afro-descendant populations, and these were much more limited in scope than those provided for indigenous peoples (Hooker 2005).

The Colombian 1991 Constitution contains several provisions on indigenous peoples' rights but only one provisional article (PA55) on Afro-descendants, which led to the adoption of Law 70 of 1993: 'In Recognition of the Right of Black Colombians to Collectively Own and Occupy their Ancestral Lands.' The differences in scope of rights for the two groups are stark. For example, constitutional law provides a quota system to guarantee two seats in the Senate (Constitution 1991, article 171) and one seat in the House of Representatives for indigenous peoples (law 649 of 2001, article 1) who officially make up 3.4 per cent of the population (DANE 2005; 2010). Conversely, Afro-descendants who make up 10.5 per cent[1] of the population are guaranteed just two seats in the House of Representatives (Law 70, article 66; Law 649, article 1).

The model minority concept is useful here for analysing the differential racialisation of Afro-descendants and indigenous peoples. Popular comparisons between the two groups often emphasise how indigenous movements have been more organised and articulated in their demands, while fractions and tensions within the Afro-descendant movement are often cited as reasons for their continued lack of success. Such distinctions fail to unpick the historical and continued differential discourses and treatment that have fed into these differences.

---

1   It is important to note that due to issues of self-identification and capacity in census taking, these figures are often considered to be underestimates of the true population size.

Framing rights claims for inclusion

The language used in the construction of rights is essential to analyse how rights are institutionalised and implemented in practice. O'Byrne asserts that through the study of the language of rights sociologists can understand the 'institutional frameworks within which meanings are negotiated and practices formalised' (2012, 832).

The 'indigenous inclusion, black exclusion' paradigm has meant that Afro-descendant communities that have gained recognition and rights tend to be those that articulate their claims within the indigenous rights framework around territory and culture (Hooker 2005).[2] Some Afro-Colombian civil society organisations point out that presenting a case based on racial discrimination can have little audience, while emphasising cultural difference is more effective (Wade 2009; Paschel 2010).

Thus, the political space that opened up through the multicultural citizenship reform made room for those groups who articulated their claims within the 'ethnic rights' language. Cultural and identity rights had long been an important demand of the Afro-Colombian movement (Pisano 2014). However, Restrepo (2013) argues that the lead up to the drafting of the Constitution involved an 'ethnicisation' of Afro-descendant claims in which organisations, mainly from the rural, Pacific region of the country had to emphasise demands for cultural, territorial and identity rights. During the actual drafting of the Constitution no Afro-descendant organisations were included in the Constitutional Committee and their interests were therefore represented by two indigenous participants and a number of anthropologists who also tended to take an ethnic rights approach (Wade 2009; Paschel 2010).

Reflecting this, PA55 and consequently Law 70 of 1993 apply to *comunidades negras* (black communities) which are defined as:

> … the group of families of Afro-Colombian descent who possesses its own culture, shares a common history and has its own traditions and customs within a rural-urban setting and which reveals and preserves a consciousness of identity that distinguishes it from other ethnic groups (Ley 70, 1993, article 2, para.5).

Thus, the law that provides rights to collective land titles, autonomy, political participation and 'ethno-education' (culturally relevant education) applied only to those Afro-descendants considered distinct, traditional ethno/cultural groups, mainly in the pacific region. This raised questions of its applicability to Afro-descendants outside of this context (Restrepo and Rojas 2012).

---

2   For example, Garífuna, communities in Central America have been successful in gaining collective titles to land through multicultural provisions in their country's constitutions (Thorne 2004; Anderson 2007).

Interest convergence

The social constructivist perspective of human rights demonstrates that political authorities institutionalise rights only when they perceive them to be in their own interests and when they do not threaten existing power structures (Waters 1996; Freeman 2002; and Miller 2010). Rights should therefore not be assumed to be automatically beneficial to the rights holders. Similarly, the CRT concept of 'interest convergence' argues that legal liberalism cannot be considered as objective, neutral or 'colour-blind.' Therefore civil rights laws and court decisions, such as rulings on desegregation or affirmative action, cannot lead to real racial justice, but rather serve wider political and economic State interests (see Bell 1995; Ladson-Billings and Tate IV 1995; Ladson-Billings 1998; Dudziak 2009; Delgado and Stefancic 2012).

In Colombia, the framing of Afro-descendant rights as rural, Pacific 'ethnic group' rights effectively enabled the State to evade obligations towards the rights of Afro-descendants who do not fit the criteria. Law 70 does extend beyond the Pacific region, for example, establishing political participation mechanisms for Black Communities from throughout the country (article 45). Further, several Constitutional Court rulings have expanded the scope of specific areas of the law.[3] However, there are still many barriers to proper implementation.

In the area of education, for example, my initial research in urban contexts demonstrates how ethno-education has been concentrated in majority Afro-descendant communities who more closely resemble a distinct ethnic group, excluding those Afro-descendants that live in more multicultural contexts. In the areas of collective land titles and participation, Afro-descendant communities face barriers realising these rights in part because their status as an 'ethnic group' had been questioned (Ng'weno 2012).[4]

After generations of neglect of Afro-Colombian ancestral territories in the Pacific region by the State, they are now the object of State and private palm oil cultivation, mining and other large-scale development projects (Murillo 2011). In the context of these neo-liberal interests, it may have suited the State to concentrate the Afro-descendant rights framework on these regions (Wade 2009). The Afro-descendant rights framework establishes mechanisms for free, prior, informed consent in development projects in the region. From an 'interest convergence' perspective this can be seen as enabling the State

3   See for example Constitutional Court rulings T-422/96 which applied education rights to black communities in the city of Santa Marta on the Caribbean Coast; and C-169/01 which expands Law 169 on political participation to include Raízal communities from San Andrés y Providencia in the definition of 'black communities'.

4   See Constitutional Court ruling T-823/12 in which a black community brought a case against the Departmental Government of Valle de Cauca for failing to fulfil their right to participation in accordance with article 45 of Law 70.

to legitimise development activities within the multiculturalist framework, effectively reconciling its neo-liberal interests with its multicultural rights obligations.

From a CRT perspective, the ethnic rights focus 'de-racialises' (Paschel 2010) Afro-descendant rights. Law 70 contains only one mention of racism (article 33) and does not specify 'any concrete proposal, sanctioning of racist acts, or clear policies' to address racism (Paschel 2010). Therefore the framework effectively denies the role that structural racism plays in the human rights violations and exclusion of Afro-Colombians.

Conclusion: using international human rights to gain domestic recognition

The consolidation of a rights framework for Afro-descendants in Colombia represents a significant advancement towards social justice, which would not have been possible without the tireless lobbying and activism by Afro-descendant civil society. However, the social constructionist and CRT frameworks enable a critical analysis of the institutionalisation of these rights, demonstrating their limitations. The restriction to 'ethnic rights' meant Afro-descendants would have to demonstrate they fit the category of an 'ethnic group' to be subjects of these rights. Further, de-racialising the rights effectively perpetuated the myth of racial democracy by denying the role that racism plays in the human rights violations of all Afro-Colombians, whether in the rural Pacific or other contexts.

Rights become institutionalised at the domestic level through a combination of State interests, pressure from social movements and the consolidation of frameworks at the international or regional levels. At the time of the adoption of the Colombian Constitution, there were no specific international or regional mechanisms on the rights of Afro-descendants. However, since the 2001 Third UN World Conference against Racism, a normative framework on the rights of Afro-descendant has begun to emerge.[5] This has expanded Afro-descendant rights from focus on traditional ethnic groups with territorial and cultural

5   This is contained in: several paragraphs in the World Conference outcome document, the Durban Declaration and Programme of Action (Declaration paras. 13–14; 32–35; and 103; and Programme of Action paras. 4–14); General Recommendation 34 on racial discrimination against people of African descent of the Committee on the Elimination of Racial Discrimination (CERD); specific mention in the Inter-American Convention against Racial Discrimination (preamble) as well as an increasing number of observations and recommendations from the CERD, the UN Working Group of Experts on People of African Descent and the Inter-American Commission's Rapporteur on the Rights of Persons of African Descent and against Racial Discrimination.

claims, to wider racial justice issues including racism in the media, racial profiling by security forces and structural discrimination.

These norms, which were largely made possible due to the activism by Latin American Afro-descendant civil society (Htun 2004; Lennox 2009), have in turn opened up new spaces for claims for racial justice at the domestic level. In this new context, anti-racism has become an increasing part of rights claims by civil society and, in 2011, Colombia adopted Law 1482 against racism and discrimination. Social media in Colombia is now abuzz with discussions on racism, linking it to wider issues of socio-economic inequality, cultural identity, territory and autonomy. This growing discourse and awareness is essential for ensuring that Afro-descendant communities can access and use legal mechanisms to make claims both for their cultural rights as ethnic groups and for racial equality by denouncing structural and institutional racism.

Bibliography

Alberti, V., and A. Araujo Pereira (2006) 'Racial discrimination in Brazil: interviews with leaders of the black movement', in *International Oral History Conference. Vol. 14.* (Sydney: IOHA).

Andrews, G. R. (2004) *Afro-Latin America, 1800–2000* (Oxford: Oxford University Press).

Bell, D. (1995) 'Racial realism', in K. Crenshaw, N. Gotanda, G. Peller and K. Thomas (eds.), *Critical Race Theory: The Key Writings That Formed the Movement* (New York: The New Press), pp. 302–12.

Constitución Política de Colombia, 1991.

Cottrol, R. J. (2001) 'The Long, Lingering Shadow: Law, Liberalism, and Cultures of Hierarchy and Identity in the Americas', *Tulane Law Review* 76, pp. 11–80.

Crenshaw, K., N. Gotanda, G. Peller and K. Thomas (eds.) (1995) *Critical Race Theory: The Key Writings That Formed the Movement* (New York: The New Press).

DANE (2005) 'Censo General 2005' (Bogotá: Departamento Administrativo Nacional de Estadísticas (DANE)).

— (2010) 'La Visibilización Estadística de Los Grupos Étnicos Colombianos'. (Bogotá: Departamento Administrativo Nacional de Estadísticas (DANE)), http://www.dane.gov.co/files/censo2005/etnia/sys/visibilidad_estadistica_etnicos.pdf.

De Friedemann, N. S. and J. Arocha (1995) 'Colombia', in P. Pérez Surday and J. Stubbs (eds.), *No Longer Invisible: Afro-Latin Americans Today* (London: Minority Rights Group International), pp. 47–76.

Delgado, R. and J. Stefancic (2012) *Critical Race Theory: An Introduction.* (2nd edn., New York and London: New York University Press).

Dudziak, M. L. (2009) 'Desegregation as a Cold War imperative', in E. Taylor, D. Gillborn and G. Ladson-Billings (eds.), *Foundations of Critical Race Theory in Education* (New York and London: Routledge), pp. 85–95.

Durban Declaration and Programme of Action (adopted at the World Conference Against Racism, Racial Discrimination, Xenophobia and Related Violence, 8 September 2001, Endorsed 15 May 2002) UNGA 56/266.

Freeman, M. (2002) *Human Rights: An Interdisciplinary Approach, Key Concepts* (Malden, MA: Polity).

Gates, Jr., H. (2011) *Black in Latin America* (New York and London: New York University Press).

Hasenbalg, C. (1996) 'Racial inequalities in Brazil and throughout Latin America: timid responses to disguised Racism', in E. Jelin and E. Hersheberg (eds.), *Constructing Democracy: Human Rights, Citizenship, and Society in Latin America* (Boulder, CO: Westview Press).

Hooker, J. (2005) 'Indigenous inclusion, black exclusion: race, ethnicity and multicultural citizenship in Latin America', *Journal of Latin American Studies* 37 (2), pp. 285–310.

Htun, M. (2004) 'From racial democracy to affirmative action: changing state policy on race in Brazil', *Latin American Research Review* 39 (1), pp. 60–89.

Hylton, K. (2012) 'Talk the talk, walk the walk: defining critical race theory in research', *Race Ethnicity and Education* 15 (1), pp. 23–41.

Hynes, P., M. Lamb, D. Short and M. Waites (eds.) (2011) *Sociology and Human Rights: New Engagements.* (Abingdon: Routledge).

Inter-American Commission on Human Rights (2011) 'The situation of people of African descent in the Americas', OEA/Ser.L/V/II, Doc. 62 (Washington DC: Organization of American States).

Ladson-Billings, G. and W. F. Tate IV (1995) 'Toward a critical race theory of education', *Teachers College Record* 97 (1), pp. 47–68.

Ladson-Billings, G. (1998) 'Just what is critical race theory and what's it doing in a nice field like education?', *International Journal of Qualitative Studies in Education* 11 (1), pp 7–24.

Leighton, K. (2012) *The Scandal of Inequality in Latin America and the Caribbean* (London: Christian Aid).

Lennox, C. (2009) 'Reviewing Durban: examining the outputs and review of the 2001 World Conference Against Racism', *Netherlands Quarterly of Human Rights* 27 (2), pp. 209–13.

Ley 70 de 1993 (27 de Agosto): Por La Cual Se Desarrolla El Artículo Transitorio 55 de La Constitución Política, Congreso de La República de Colombia.

Ley 649 de 2001 (marzo 27): Por La Cual Se Reglamenta El Artículo 176 de La Constitución Política de Colombia. El Congreso de La República de Colombia.

Ley 1482 de 2011 (noviembre 30): Por Medio de La Cual Se Modifica El Código Penal Y Se Establecen Otras Disposiciones. El Congreso de La República de Colombia. n.d.

Miller, H. (2010) 'From 'rights-based' to 'rights-framed' approaches: a social constructionist view of human rights practice', *The International Journal of Human Rights* 14 (6), pp. 915–31.

Morris, L. (ed.) (2006) *Rights: Sociological Perspectives* (Abingdon: Routledge).

Morrison, J. (2012) 'Social movements in Latin America: the power of regional and national networks', in K. Dixon and J. Burdick (eds.), *Comparative Perspectives on Afro-Latin America* (Gainesville, FL: University Press of Florida), pp. 243–63.

Murillo, P. (2011) 'El Tercer Laboratorio de La Paz Y La Población Afrocolombiana', *Acción Social.*

Ng'weno, B. (2012) 'Beyond citizenship as we know it: race and ethnicity in Afro-Colombian struggles for citizenship equality', in K. Dixon and J. Burdick (eds.), *Comparative Perspectives on Afro-Latin America* (Gainesville, FL: University Press of Florida), pp. 156–75.

O'Byrne, D. (2012) 'On the sociology of human rights: theorising the language-structure of rights', *Sociology* 46 (5), pp. 829–43.

Omi, M. and H. Winant (1994) *Racial Formation in the United States: From the 1960s to the 1990s* (Abingdon: Routledge).

Paschel, T. S. (2010) 'The right to difference: explaining Colombia's shift from color blindness to the law of black communities', *American Journal of Sociology* 116 (3), pp. 729–69.

Pisano, P. (2014) 'Movilidad Social E Identidad 'negra' En La Segunda Mitad Del Siglo Xx: Social mobility and 'black' identity in the second half of the 20th century', *Anuario Colombiano de Historia Social Y de La Cultura* 41 (1), pp. 179–99.

Reichmann, R. (1999) *Race in Contemporary Brazil: From Indifference to Inequality* (University Park, PA: The Pennsylvania State University Press).

Restrepo, E. (2013) *Etnización de La Negritud: La Invención de Las "Comunidades Negras" Como Grupo Etnico En Colombia.* Genealogias de La Negritud (Popayán: Editorial Universidad de Cauca).

Restrepo, E. and A. Rojas (2012) 'Políticas Currículares En Tiempos de Multiculturalismo: Proyectos Educativos De/para Afrodescendientes En Colombia', *Currículo Sem Fronteiras* 12 (1), pp. 157–73.

Safa, H. (1998) 'Race and national identity in the Americas', *Latin American Perspectives* 25 (3), pp. 3–12.

Samson, D. and D. Short (2006) 'Sociology of indigenous peoples rights', in L. Morris (ed.), *Rights: Sociological Perspectives* (Abingdon: Routledge).

Sanchez, M. and M. Bryan (2003) *Macro Study: Afro-Descendants, Discrimination and Economic Exclusion in Latin America* (London: Minority Rights Group International).

Sieder, R. (2002) *Multiculturalism in Latin America: Indigenous Rights, Diversity and Democracy* (Basingstoke: Palgrave Macmillan).

Short, D. (2007) 'The social construction of indigenous "native title" land rights in Australia', *Current Sociology* 55 (6), pp. 857–76.

Taylor, E., D. Gillborn and G. Ladson-Billings (eds.) (2009) *Foundations of Critical Race Theory in Education* (New York: Routledge).

Telles, E. (2004) *Race in Another America: The Significance of Skin Color in Brazil* (Princeton, NJ: Princeton University Press).

— (2014) *Pigmentocracies: Ethnicity, Race, and Color in Latin America* (Chapel Hill, NC: University of North Carolina Press).

UN Committee on the Elimination of Racial Discrimination (2011), *General Recommendation No 34 on Racial Discrimination against People of African Descent*, UN Doc. CERD/C/GC/34. (30 September 2011).

UNDP (2012) *Análisis de La Situación Socioeconómica de La Población Afroperuana Y de La Población Afrocostarricense Y Su Comparación Con La Situación de Las Poblaciones Afrocolombiana Y Afroecuatoriana*. (Panamá: United Nations Development Programme).

Wade, P. (2009) 'Defining Blackness in Colombia', *Journal de La Société Des Américanistes* 95 (1), pp. 165–84.

— (2004) 'Images of Latin American Mestizaje and the politics of comparison', *Bulletin of Latin American Research* 23 (3), pp. 355–66.

— (1997) *Race and Ethnicity in Latin America* (London & Chicago: Pluto Press).

Waters, M. (1996) 'Human rights and universalisation of interests: towards a social constructionist approach', *Sociology* 30 (3), pp. 593–600.

5

Bringing human rights home: refugees, reparation, and the responsibility to protect

James Souter

Human rights, it is often observed, have become a common global language for making moral claims. One consequence of this is that there is a huge range of ways in which states, organisations and other actors draw on, invoke and mobilise human rights in different locations and contexts. The vast array of campaigns, treaties, laws and policies which fall under the umbrella of human rights means that human rights talk will be continually contested and, to some extent, fragmented, contradictory, and inconsistent. In Richard Wilson's phrase, human rights discourse will remain strongly marked by 'ideological promiscuity' (Wilson 2006). Given that human rights talk and practice are partly shaped by power, these inconsistencies will inevitably, at least to some degree, reflect power relations and dominant interests within and across states.

The existence of inconsistencies in some of the ways in which human rights are framed and put into practice has become more and more apparent to me in the years since I completed the MA in Understanding and Securing Human Rights in 2009. Liberal democratic states, such as the UK, profess their strong commitment to human rights principles. However, such states seem to tend towards the view that much of the business of human rights protection is something that should, or even can, only or mainly be provided beyond their borders. As Dan Bulley (2010, 43) has discussed, debates in such states often construct the 'human' in human rights as a subject which can 'only be saved close to its territorially qualified home', placing human rights squarely within the realm of foreign policy. When it comes to opening up the state to refugees, however, this commitment to human rights can come dangerously close to evaporating, given the range of measures used by Western states to prevent the arrival of asylum seekers and to limit the numbers of refugees they protect. This, it appears to me, is evident when we consider both efforts to achieve reparation and accountability for the harms suffered by refugees, and the ways in which states have framed the 'responsibility to protect' and sought to put it into practice. For the promise of human rights to be truly realised, I will suggest, reparation for refugees and the responsibility to protect need to be fully 'brought home' to liberal democratic states and linked to the practice of granting asylum to refugees.

Reparation and refugees

Reparation – whether in the form of restitution, compensation or satisfaction – is affirmed in international human rights treaties, and by the UN General Assembly, which adopted the Reparations Guidelines in 2005.[1] Article 2 of the International Covenant on Civil and Political Rights (1966), for instance, lays down a right to 'an effective remedy' for violations of the human rights therein. Refugees, fleeing as they often do from severe violations of human rights and being subjected to serious harm during perilous journeys, are clearly entitled to such reparation. However, where reparation has been linked to refugee protection in theory and practice, it has largely been in relation to refugees' states of origin, and in the context of their repatriation (e.g. Bradley 2013; Cantor 2011). This is *partly* appropriate, for many of the harms of displacement are perpetrated by refugees' states of origin or by non-state actors within those states, and voluntary repatriation and reparations processes within these states – such as compensation, property restitution or truth-telling – can be the most fitting way of remedying the harms that refugees suffer.

It is a mistake, however, to assume that this is always the case. The static conception of protection as something that is possible only at, or near to, home has been reflected in what B.S. Chimni (1998, 360) has dubbed an 'internalist' approach to the causes of forced migration, which assumes that refugees' states of origin are entirely or mainly responsible for refugees' flight. Yet this internalist view ignores the clearly *external* causes of many contemporary cases of forced migration, whether as a result of military interventions, support for oppressive regimes, or the imposition of damaging economic policies. Interventions by Western states in Vietnam, Kosovo, Iraq and Libya in the past half-century, for instance, have produced huge numbers of refugees.

Once these external causes of displacement are brought into view, it becomes much less clear why reparation is something that is owed only within refugees' states of origin. As I have argued elsewhere, reparation for refugees is at times owed by states in the form of *asylum* (Souter 2014). When it comes to responsibilities towards refugees, the principle of reparation is often as applicable to refugees' host states as it is to their states of origin. There is, however, little evidence that the implications of the principle of reparation for

1   United Nations General Assembly (2005), *Basic Principles and Guidelines on the Right to a Remedy and Reparation for Victims of Gross Violations of International Law and Serious Violations of International Humanitarian Law*, UN Doc. A/RES/60/147 (21 March 2006), available at http://www.un.org/ga/search/view_doc.asp?symbol=A/RES/60/147 (accessed 27 August 2015).

asylum are recognised by states, save for a few isolated initiatives. In any case, these have tended to prioritise refugees who have assisted external states in their interventions, such as Iraqi and Afghan translators and interpreters who have worked for the US and UK, rather than offering asylum as reparation more broadly to those displaced by the receiving state's own actions.

The responsibility to protect

While refugee protection has been an important part of the human rights culture that has developed since World War Two, humanitarian intervention has remained a more controversial means of potentially upholding human rights in grave humanitarian emergencies. Drawing on existing human rights and humanitarian law, states unanimously agreed at the UN General Assembly in 2005 that they bear a 'responsibility to protect' (R2P) populations from genocide, ethnic cleansing, war crimes and crimes against humanity. This is primarily a responsibility of states to protect their own citizens, but it also involves assisting other states to fulfil their R2P, as well as, in the language of the World Summit Outcome Document, taking 'collective action, in a timely and decisive manner' when states are 'manifestly failing' to protect their populations from these four crimes.[2] This may, but need not necessarily, involve military intervention.

As with the matter of reparation for refugees, R2P is generally viewed in liberal democratic states primarily as a foreign policy issue. In other words, although R2P has its roots in the same human rights tradition as refugee protection and reparation, they are not generally viewed holistically. While the tendency to conflate R2P with military intervention to protect human rights has been dwindling in recent years, and a wider range of preventive activities – including, for instance, early-warning systems alerting states to impending atrocities – have been placed under the banner of R2P, it is nevertheless still predominantly viewed as something that 'we' do 'over there', in far-off states wracked by violence.

Yet the implications of R2P for states' asylum policies are not difficult to make out. When atrocities are imminent or are already being committed, a very frequent response by people at risk is to flee. R2P is meant to protect individuals at risk from these atrocities, and an obvious means of doing so is through offers of asylum (Barbour and Gorlick 2008; Welsh 2014). While there is a strong case for seeing asylum as a core element of R2P as a matter of course, making this linkage becomes even more important when the traditional understanding of R2P as humanitarian intervention is an obstacle to the delivery of effective

2　United Nations General Assembly (2005), *World Summit Outcome Document*, 15 September, UN Doc. A/RES/60/1 (24 October 2005), paras. 138 and 139, p. 30, available at http://www.un.org/womenwatch/ods/A-RES-60–1–E.pdf (accessed 27 August 2015).

protection to those at risk. Military action is not only dangerous – risking as it does inflaming already volatile situations yet further and creating a fresh round of refugees who are owed reparation – but it is not always politically possible, given that it may be vetoed at the UN Security Council, or voted down in national parliaments, as we have seen in relation to the on-going crisis in Syria.

The international community's inaction in the face of atrocities committed as part of the Syrian civil war since 2011 has led some commentators to point to the failure – or even untimely death – of R2P. Yet this view betrays an overly narrow understanding of what R2P is and entails. Only if R2P is solely a matter of foreign policy does the current impasse over the crisis in Syria signify R2P's demise. In response to this deadlock, states can approach R2P creatively and make the obvious links with the alternative of asylum (Gilgan 2015). Rather than leaving the responsibility to protect Syrian refugees to already overburdened neighbouring states, such as Turkey, European states can partly discharge their own R2P to many of those refugees who are now in any case seeking to enter Europe in large numbers.

Linking R2P with the principle of reparation can also potentially help to make some headway in making R2P's vision a reality. When R2P falls on other states to step in when states are 'manifestly failing' to fulfil their primary responsibility to their citizens, the fact that R2P is seen by states as a general responsibility, that is shared equally among all states, creates a collective action problem. This view of R2P as a diffuse, shared responsibility allows each state to claim to uphold R2P while not seeing it as *its* specific role to take action in any given situation. Assigning a special responsibility to protect to a particular state or states on the basis of the principle of reparation when there is a case for doing so can help to overcome this problem, and to ensure that effective action is taken to protect those at risk from atrocities (see Pattison 2010; Tan 2006). For instance, as I have recently argued in an article with Jason Ralph, given that the 2003 invasion of Iraq destroyed the Iraqi state and rendered Iraqis highly vulnerable to external shock, which then materialised in the form of Islamic State in 2014, it is reasonable to argue that the US and other states which took part in the invading coalition, such as the UK and Australia, bear a 'special responsibility to protect' that is more demanding than a merely general responsibility shared with all states, and includes an obligation to offer asylum to a larger number of Iraqi refugees (Ralph and Souter 2015).

Thinking 'outside the box'

There is a broader point to be made here about how academics study human rights, and the role of political frameworks and policy categories in their research. Many scholars in human rights and refugee studies are motivated by a desire to alleviate suffering and injustice, and are concerned to ensure that their research has a positive impact on efforts to protect human rights, by raising awareness or influencing policy. In order to gain policy relevance, understandably academics often speak in the language that politicians and policy-makers understand. In doing so, however, there is a danger that they replicate and reinforce artificial divisions between elements of human rights law, policy and practice, such as those concerning reparation, asylum and R2P that I have highlighted here, that are more reflective of states' interests than the needs of those at risk or the situations in which they find themselves. There is a danger that the uncritical use of policy categories can distort research on human rights and refugees, and limit its progressive potential (see Bakewell 2008; Turton 2003). Scholars, for instance, have largely left unchallenged the view that reparation for refugees is a matter for refugees' states of origin, or the idea that R2P is solely or largely a foreign policy issue. The desire for policy relevance needs to be coupled with a critical approach to policy categories and frameworks. Only then can academics and researchers help to overcome the inconsistencies and blind spots that currently beset some of the current efforts to understand and promote human rights.

Bibliography

Bakewell, O. (2008) 'Research beyond the categories: the importance of policy irrelevant research into forced migration', *Journal of Refugee Studies* 21 (4), pp. 432–453.

Barbour, B. and B. Gorlick (2008) 'Embracing the "responsibility to protect": a repertoire of measures including asylum for potential victims', *International Journal of Refugee Law* 20 (4), pp. 533–66.

Bradley, M. (2013) *Refugee Repatriation. Justice, Responsibility and Redress* (Cambridge: Cambridge University Press).

Bulley, D. (2010) 'Home is where the human is? Ethics, intervention and hospitality in Kosovo', *Millennium: Journal of International Studies* 39 (1), pp. 43–63.

Cantor, D. J. (2011) 'Restitution, Compensation, Satisfaction: Transnational Reparations and Colombia's Victims' Law', *UNHCR Working Paper No. 215.* (Geneva: UNHCR).

Chimni, B. S. (1998) 'The geo-politics of refugee studies: a view from the South', *Journal of Refugee Studies* 11 (4), pp. 350–374.

Gilgan, C. (2015) *Lost in Translation? The Responsibility to Protect, the UK and Syrian Refugees.* Presented at the Postgraduate Research Conference, School of Politics and International Studies, University of Leeds, 10 June.

Pattison, J. (2010) *Humanitarian Intervention and the Responsibility to Protect. Who Should Intervene?* (Oxford: Oxford University Press).

Ralph, J.G. and J. Souter (2015) 'A special responsibility to protect: The UK, Australia, and the rise of Islamic State', *International Affairs* 91 (4), pp. 709–724.

Souter, J. (2015) 'Why the UK has a special responsibility to protect its share of refugees', *The Conversation* (15 May 2015).

Souter, J. (2014) 'Towards a theory of asylum as reparation for past injustice', *Political Studies* 62 (2), pp. 326–42.

Tan, K-C. (2006) 'The Duty to Protect', in T. Nardin and M. S. Williams (eds.), *NOMOS XLVII: Humanitarian Intervention* (New York: New York University Press).

Turton, D. (2003) 'Conceptualising forced migration', *Refugee Studies Centre Working Paper No. 12* (Oxford: Refugee Studies Centre).

Welsh, J. (2014) 'Fortress Europe and the R2P: framing the issue', presented at *The Lampedusa Dilemma: Global Flows and Closed Borders. What Should Europe Do?*, European University Institute, Florence, Italy, 17–18 November 2014.

Wilson, R.A. (2006) 'Afterword to "Anthropology and Human Rights in a New Key": the social life of human rights', *American Anthropologist* 108 (1), pp. 77–83.

6

Human rights and the new(ish) digital paradigm

Gaia Marcus

To call the internet and its accompanied increase in computing capabilities a 'new' phenomenon would be something of a misnomer – the internet has been in development since the 1960s, and became publically available in August 1991. However, the globalisation of communications, associated erosion in state borders and dizzying acceleration of technological advancement over the past two decades have fundamentally changed the citizen-state relationship, introducing new actors, new platforms, new opportunities and new threats.

Whilst it is beyond the scope of the chapter to define this new(ish) digital paradigm, several characteristics are highlighted. First, the weakening of the nation state both as a concept and as a geographical entity with borders that can be protected physically. Second, the ascendance of new global actors that dwarf nation states in budget, reach and technological know-how. Third, the creation of a globalised communications infrastructure (the internet!) that is multi-channel and subject to rapid flux. Fourth, the exponential increase in computing capabilities, which opens up new possibilities for data capture and analysis- from big data to social network analysis. As noted by Kaku 'Today, your cell phone has more computer power than all of NASA back in 1969, when it placed two astronauts on the moon' (2011, 21). This (thoroughly incomplete) chapter is intended to stimulate further thought and debate with regards to applying this new(ish) digital paradigm to our understanding of human rights and the ways in which human rights defenders implement programmes and hold states and other actors to account.

Digital human rights?

The concept of digital rights tends to encompass how the new(ish) digital paradigm adds new dimensions to existing rights, and this will be the focus of the following section. A separate area of enquiry (not touched upon here) is examining whether new rights are created by the new(ish) digitised paradigm in which we live. For example, what would a 'right to the Internet' look like?

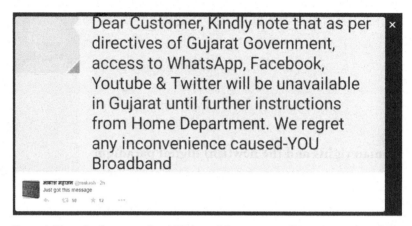

Figure 1. Example of state mandated blocking of the internet in Gujarat; screenshot of picture shared on Twitter taken by author, all identifying information has been removed. See BBC (2015).

There is precedent: internet access is now protected in certain legal systems (Lucchi 2011). Similarly, individuals' right to access information 'regardless of frontiers' is currently a subset of Article 19 of the Universal Declaration of Human Rights (UDHR). What might a 'right to access information' look like as a right in and of itself given the 'massive blocking, throttling, and filtering of the internet'[1] and the impact this has upon citizens?

Digital rights: some usual suspects

For Souter (2012) the articles most commonly understood by human rights professionals as being affected by the internet are articles 18, 19 and 20 of the UDHR – the rights to freedom of conscience, expression and association, respectively.

In the positive, it is now easier to share and access information, with more and easier channels for disseminating information and views. The right to association can now also be a virtual right, with exchange happening across borders, using mediums ranging from text messaging to teleconferences. The current Syrian refugee crisis and the Mediterranean crisis have seen both refugees using Facebook forums to understand where it is safe to pass and where to go, and European citizens using Facebook, Twitter and other online forums to self-organise and respond.

---

1   United Nations Office of the High Commissioner for Human Rights, *Human rights, encryption and anonymity in a digital age* (1 July 2015). Available at http://www.ohchr.org/EN/NewsEvents/Pages/HRencryptionanonymityinadigitalage.aspx#sthash.FmDjxYec.dpuf (accessed 9 Oct. 2015).

In the negative, an increased reliance on digital channels risks exacerbating the marginalisation of those without the digital or technical literacy to participate, or even the linguistics or literacy skills to navigate a mainly text-based interface. For example, moves to shift online all job listings or voting systems, or access to state services such as health or pensions, greatly affect those who cannot (or do not wish to) use such platforms.

Online threats, offline impacts

New technologies are leading to new and increasingly more covert ways in which these rights can be curtailed. These include the blocking and intercepting of communications and channels (Figure 1), and can entail wholesale interception of all communications. While this is in theory possible with any remote method of communication – from intercepting post to scrambling radio signals – digital methods mean that far more can be done with far less man-power.

Online threats to rights such as the freedom of expression can have far more serious offline repercussions to human rights defenders and citizens given the enhanced potential for surveillance and locating actors using digital methods. These, sometimes deadly, threats can come from both state and non-state perpetrators. A recent case involved Mexican militia locating human rights defenders who were active online using both social media and offline pressure. The murder of the Mexican *Valor por Tamaulipas* journalist featured a particularly gruesome twist: her own social media accounts were used to announce and broadcast her murder (BBC 2014). Where states are involved, online surveillance can lead to mass state suppression, such as following the 'Arab Spring' in Egypt (McPherson and Alexander 2014). The very threat to life and basic freedoms places new responsibilities on human rights defenders and other actors, as the UN Special Rapporteur on freedom of opinion and expression, David Kaye, highlights:

> We live in a world in which mass and targeted surveillance, digital attacks on individuals and civil society, harassment of members of vulnerable groups, and a wide variety of digital opinion and expression result in serious repercussions, including detention, physical attacks, and even killings.[2]

Digital rights: some more unusual suspects

New channels lead to new ways in which rights can be violated, some of which may not be obvious at first. For example, the rights to non-discrimination and to a free and fair participation in society are at risk. Further, data protection and the right to privacy and private life are ever more at risk from excessive

2   Ibid.

state surveillance and a largely unchecked global data-farming industry that is far more advanced in its science than most national governments (Venkataramanan 2015).

A tyranny of algorithms?

An overlooked, but potentially fertile line of inquiry would be the way in which the internet affects the right to non-discrimination: enter the algorithm.

Almost everything that you see on a responsive website – a website where content is not static, but tailored to the user – is a result of an increasingly complex set of algorithms. They tend to be geared towards efficiency, which often means revenue. This is why sites such as Amazon recommend new purchases or books to you, and explains why you are followed around the internet by adverts displaying products you have recently viewed. It affects your search results, the news you see, your experience of social media and much more.

A recent Google scandal highlighted what this means in practice. Datta, Tschantz and Datta (2014) found that men were shown adverts that advertised roles with large salaries more frequently than women. It is unclear from the research 'where' the gender based discrimination 'occurred', whether within the advertiser preferences themselves or within the way in which internet users were selected by Google to view the adverts. What the case did highlight, however, is the way in which algorithms can tend towards re-trenching existing inequalities and associated discrimination. In this case there was a retrenchment of societal trends leading to men being more highly paid than women, but the basic mechanics are applicable to any bias that has its basis in social structures.

Recent cases have highlighted how online targeting and interactions – driven again by algorithms – can have offline repercussions. Facebook, for example, is able to increase voting in a geographical area through increasing the visibility of others having voted. Whilst an experiment that increases voting may seem like no bad thing, imagine the consequence to our right to free and fair elections if this targeting only happened in areas where a certain political party was particularly strong. There should be more attention paid to what we see on the internet, and the decision making processes or algorithms behind it. Nothing we see online is 'neutral' and more scrutiny needs to be placed on the human rights implications of that.

Too boring to fight for?

The technicality of the debate can be a key barrier to human rights activists and scholars truly engaging with the new(ish) digital paradigm. Concepts such as 'net neutrality' – the idea that it should not be possible to make it easier or cheaper to access certain parts of the internet – have key repercussions on our ability to use the internet for free expression and association. For example, the

European Commission (2015) currently highlights the way in which service providers slow down (or 'throttle') service on free Voice over Internet services, e.g. Skype, pushing traffic to paid for services. The way in which service providers or states (e.g. see Figure 1) are able to control platforms that are used by citizens for association and communication is clearly worthy of further analysis.

The right to privacy, contained within Article 12 of the UDHR, is another field of study that is currently limited to more technologically literate commentators and campaigners (Bélanger and Crossler 2011), or those specialising in information law and related disciplines. However, this could be an interesting area for further research, especially by researchers approaching it from a more conceptual angle. Indeed, the right to privacy is now a key area where balancing competing rights and principles such as proportionality come to the fore.

Civil society groups such as the UK 'Open Rights Group' or 'European Digital Rights' will focus on the ways in which online surveillance curtails rights. However, some element of state surveillance of communications could now be seen as being a fundamental component of states preserving fundamental rights and public order. What might the correct approach be towards derogating from certain rights? How have these played out in different regimes? Further analysis could shed interesting light: why do some states take a permissive line such as Germany's, and others a state surveillance heavy line such as the UK? Indeed, while the German Federal Constitutional Court ruled against the legality of 'the state [collecting] computerised data about a section of the population [...] in order to identify potential subjects for surveillance' in 2006 (Youngs 2008, 331), the UK's position has led the UN Human Rights Committee to recently recommend that the UK 'should review its counter-terrorism legislation in order to bring it into line with its obligations under the Covenant.'[3]

Acting and holding actors to account

The new(ish) digital paradigm affords human rights defenders and scholars with new ways to hold duty bearers to account and fight for the completion of rights. These can range from the methods used to evaluate whether rights are being infringed, and how, to new awareness raising mechanisms; for example, using websites such as http://www.eyesondarfur.org, or the current trend for petitions and associated 'clicktivism', or using very widespread web tools such as Facebook to respond to humanitarian crises.

3   United Nations Human Rights Committee (2015). *Concluding observations on the seventh periodic report of the United Kingdom of Great Britain and Northern Ireland* (advance unedited version) (Geneva: United Nations), available at http://www. equalityhumanrights.com/sites/default/files/uploads/Pdfs/CCPR_C_GBR_CO_7. pdf (accessed 9 Oct. 2015).

Using quantitative data analysis to hold states to account

The statistical analysis of large datasets can offer insight as to the fulfilment of rights at a local, regional, national and international level. For example, the Centrepoint Youth Homelessness Databank project is creating an open data source for the UK about youth homelessness. The aspiration is to collect all available data on youth homelessness, open the data up using an interactive website, and perform analyses using it. This will allow insight into how rights to housing are being fulfilled, and if there are any specific demographic groups who are most affected by homelessness.

Compiling and aggregating data is a useful way of contrasting official statistics and rhetoric, and trying to delve into the problem at hand. A little data can go a long way. With incomplete data, collected through a Freedom of Information request, the databank showed that eight times more young people ask the state for help in England and Wales than those who are officially being supported with housing by the state – this is equivalent to 136,000 young people seeking support and only 16,000 accessing their full legal entitlement to housing. This suggests that a significant majority of young people at risk of or experiencing homelessness in England and Wales are not adequately accessing their 'right to a standard of living adequate for [their] health and well-being', as per Article 25 of the UDHR.

Using network analysis to understand power structures?

Network analysis is a way of identifying actors and analysing the ties between them: kinship, friendship, reporting relationships, money flows and so on. Skye Bender-deMoll (2008) provides an excellent overview of the types of relationship that can be studied and some network basics. The RSA (Royal Society of Arts) has carried out extensive work on using network analysis to understand marginalised communities, identifying key actors and then working with them to plan local interventions (Rowson et al. 2010; Marcus 2011).

As a tool, network analysis allows the researcher to shed light on some of the key tenets of the human rights based approach: understanding underlying power structures; highlighting who the most disenfranchised are; and schematising how the intervention will affect social and other structures. Further, when analysing human rights violations, it is critical to understand the relationship between various actors and the networks of command or control that underpinned them.

Whilst network analysis is a burgeoning field in its own right, it can often feel daunting and time consuming to the newcomer. New tools that use tablet computers to store, code and analyse the data, even without internet access are becoming more viable. Any human rights scholar interested in pursuing this further should look into two open-source projects currently looking for collaborators: Rand Corporations 'EgoWeb' project or the University of Kentucky's 'OpenEddi' project.

Crowd-sourcing data and social media research

The ability to crowd-source a large amount of data, rapidly, can lead to better project planning, implementation, evaluation and monitoring. Live data can be used to understand where problems are worse, to track ongoing progress and to evaluate change over time. Sourcing data from social media can be used to hold duty bearers to account, for example, mapping human rights violations or humanitarian crises.

The Ushaidi project, for example, was initially deployed in Kenya in 2008 to map reports of post-election violence that were compiled from individual text messages and verified. The Peta Jakarta project, whilst using a similar method of collecting, verifying and mapping citizen reports (this time through Twitter), is used by Jakartan authorities and citizens alike to map flooding and make decisions on resource allocation and disaster responses based on real-time data.

Whilst the potential for using big data sources such as social media is clear, the ethics of using social media data are far murkier (McPherson and Alexander 2014). What does informed consent look like? How far can we trust the data – verifying reports is complicated, costly and sometimes inconclusive? Is it justifiable to collate and keep data without specific consent from the data subjects?

More starkly, what do we do with the data we are collecting: might we be putting people at risk through poor encryption or anonymisation (see McPherson 2014, and the Human Rights in the Digital Age project)?[4] This problem is at all levels: as highlighted by the UN Special Rapporteur on freedom of opinion and expression, there is currently no safe way of individuals contacting the UN to report violations.[5] Human rights institutions do need to play technological catch-up to retain their relevance.

Human first, digital second

This chapter has provided an incomplete overview of questions and challenges when applying our new(ish) digital paradigm to the international human rights regime. It has been squarely based on my own expertise and context, without seeking to look at the bleeding edge or darker corners of technology:

4   Centre for Governance and Human Rights, *Human Rights in the Digital Age*, available at http://www.cghr.polis.cam.ac.uk/research-themes/human-rights-in-the-digital-age-1 (accessed 8 Oct. 2015).

5   United Nations Human Rights Council, *Report of the Special Rapporteur on the promotion and protection of the right to freedom of opinion and expression, David Kaye*, UN Doc. A/HRC/29/32 (22 May 2015).

block chain technology, artificial intelligence, semantic or natural language processing, drones, the dark web, and others.

I have suggested some avenues for investigating digital rights, and new methods that can be used to both analyse the fulfilment of human rights and to hold rights bearers to account. This is a field in constant flux, and a field that sorely needs more scrutiny from those interested in the human first, digital second. Please do join us!

Bibliography

BBC (2014) *#BBCtrending: Murdered for tweeting in Mexico?* (27 October 2014), available at http://www.bbc.co.uk/news/magazine-29746651 (accessed 8 Oct. 2015).

BBC (2015) *Why has India blocked mobile internet messaging?* (27 August 2015), available at http://www.bbc.co.uk/news/blogs-trending-34074466 (accessed 8 Oct. 2015).

Belanger, F. and R. E. Crossler (2011) 'Privacy in the digital age: a review of information privacy research in information systems', *MIS Quarterly* 35 (4), pp. 1017–41.

Bender-deMoll, S. (2008) *Potential Human Rights Uses of Network Analysis and Mapping – A report to the Science and Human Rights Program of the American Association for the Advancement of Science*, available at http://skyeome.net/wordpress/wp-content/uploads/2008/05/Net_Mapping_Report.pdf (accessed 8 Oct. 2015).

Centre for Governance and Human Rights, *Human Rights in the Digital Age*, available at http://www.cghr.polis.cam.ac.uk/research-themes/human-rights-in-the-digital-age-1 (accessed 8 Oct. 2015).

Datta, A., M. C. Tschantz and A. Datta (2014) *Automated Experiments on Ad Privacy Settings: A Tale of Opacity, Choice, and Discrimination*, available at http://www.degruyter.com/view/j/popets.2015.1.issue-1/popets-2015–0007/popets-2015–0007.xml (accessed 8 Oct. 2015).

European Commission (2015) *Net Neutrality Challenges*, available at https://ec.europa.eu/digital-agenda/en/net-neutrality-challenges#Article (accessed 8 Oct. 2015).

Kaku, M. (2011) *Physics of the Future: How Science Will Shape Human Destiny and Our Daily Lives by the Year 2100* (New York: Doubleday).

Lucchi, N. (2011) 'Access to network services and protection of constitutional rights: recognizing the essential role of internet access for the freedom of expression', *Cardozo Journal of International and Comparative Law* 19 (3), pp. 645–78.

Marcus, G., T. Newmark and S. Broome (2011) *Power Lines* (London: RSA).

McPherson, E. (2014) *Human Rights in the Digital Age* (video) (Cambridge: Centre of Governance and Human Rights, University of Cambridge), available at http://www.cghr.polis.cam.ac.uk/research-themes/human-rights-in-the-digital-age-1 (accessed 15 Oct. 2015).

McPherson, E. and A. Alexander (2014) *Written Evidence for the Social Media Data and Real Time Analytics Inquiry* (London: Science and Technology Committee (Commons)), available at https://www.academia.edu/7621298/Written_evidence_submitted_to_the_Science_and_Technology_Committee_Commons_for_the_inquiry_on_social_media_data_and_real_time_analytics (accessed 15 Oct. 2015).

Rowson, J., S. Broome and A. Jones (2010) *Connected Communities: How social networks power and sustain the Big Society* (London: RSA).

Souter, D. (2012) *Human Rights and the Internet: A review of perceptions of human rights organisations. Report to the Association for Progressive Communications*, available at https://www.apc.org/en/system/files/HumanRightsAndTheInternet_20120627.pdf (accessed 15 Oct. 2015).

United Nations Human Rights Committee (2015) *Concluding observations on the seventh periodic report of the United Kingdom of Great Britain and Northern Ireland* (Geneva: United Nations), available at http://www.equalityhumanrights.com/sites/default/files/uploads/documents/humanrights/UN/CCPRC%20GB%20concluding%20observations%20(1).pdf (accessed 15 Oct. 2015).

United Nations Human Rights Council (2015) *Report of the Special Rapporteur on the promotion and protection of the right to freedom of opinion and expression, David Kaye*, UN Doc. A/HRC/29/32 (22 May 2015).

United Nations Office of the High Commissioner for Human Rights (2015) *Human rights, encryption and anonymity in a digital age* (1 July 2015), available at http://www.ohchr.org/EN/NewsEvents/Pages/HRencryptionanonymityinadigitalage.aspx#sthash.FmDjxYec.dpuf (accessed 9 Oct. 2015).

Venkataramanan, M. (2015) 'Revealed: How free apps eavesdrop on your entire private life', *Wired* (14 July 2015), available at http://www.wired.co.uk/magazine/archive/2015/08/start/infoporn-free-apps-are-giving-away-your-private-life (accessed 8 Oct. 2015).

Youngs, R. (2008) 'Germany: shooting down aircraft and analyzing computer data', *International Journal of Constitutional Law* 6 (2), pp. 331–48.

Websites and avenues

https://www.openrightsgroup.org
https://edri.org

http://www.eyesondarfur.org

http://www.rand.org/methods/egoweb.html

University of Kentucky OpenEddi- http://www.uky.edu/publichealth/about/
faculty-and-staff-directory/kate-eddens

http://www.valorportamaulipas.info

http://www.ushahidi.com

http://petajakarta.org/banjir/en/

Part 2

Securing Human Rights

7

Theories of change for human rights and for development[1]

Paul Gready

Few human rights agencies work with an explicit theory of change. It is much more common for agencies to have an implicit, partially formed theory of change. Eyben et al. (2008, 202–3) place an 'archetypes framework' in this category – change is implicitly thought to come about through some taken-for-granted conventional wisdom (enlightened elites, new laws, people in the streets, a good example, a shock to the system, etc.). The objective of this chapter is to explore what might be gained by bringing these implicit, partially formed theories of change to light within human rights practice.

A theory of change sets out 'underlying assumptions about the relationships between desired outcomes and the way proposed interventions are expected to *bring them about*' (Aragón and Macedo 2010, 89, italics in the original). Developing a theory of change can be perceived as producing an *output* that describes how activities lead to outcomes, or as a *process* with an emphasis on conceptual thinking and on-going reflection or learning designed to articulate and interrogate the relationship between activities and outcomes. A good theory of change provides a specific and measurable description of a social change initiative that forms the basis for strategic planning, decision-making, evaluation and on-going processes of learning. It is important to note that theories of change can apply to a specific project or programme, an organisation's approach or philosophy, a wider collaborative campaign or policy initiative, and the impacts of an entire field such as transitional justice or humanitarian assistance. 'Systemic' theories of change are underpinned by the idea that 'there ought to be a systemic relationship between our understanding of the conditions that are needed for social change *to be able to* emerge in a given context, and the 'internal,' organisational conditions that might best allow us to support that change' (Aragón and Macedo 2010, 91). The breadth of understandings of theories of change in development, where such theories

---

1 This chapter draws on the following publications: Gready and Vandenhole (eds.) (2014) and Vandenhole and Gready (2014).

are well advanced, range from perceiving them as a highly technical planning tool linked to a donor-driven 'results agenda' – for example, an extension of the assumptions made in a logframe– to a participatory and politicised approach to understanding how particular actions impact on sets of power relations to yield impacts. As such, theories of change are understood in very different ways, and play various roles in practice.

This chapter compares human rights and development theories of change for a number of reasons. As noted above, theories of change in development are more advanced, originating in the literature on monitoring and evaluation. In human rights practice, theories of change are virtually non-existent. Will human rights feel the need to articulate theories of change? If so, will organisations simply borrow from neighbours such as development organisations or generate their own theories of change? Whatever transferable lessons there may be one would also expect differences between the two fields to be reflected in their theories of change, despite recent convergence brought about by more serious work on economic and social rights, human rights-based approaches to development, etc. Development work is essentially evidence based, for example moving forward from concrete problems and dilemmas, whereas human rights activism is more usually governed by laws and norms (as such human rights practice often starts from laws and works backwards). Development actors frequently work in partnership with governments, and in some cases will work with governments which human rights agencies regard as oppressive. Such differences will surely inform theories of change. In sum, development work has traditionally been more evidence based, preventive, pragmatic, and non-confrontational, while human rights work is still norm-based, principle-led, and more reactive and adversarial.

Five entry-points to theories of change are addressed in this chapter: 1) The state. 2) The law. 3) Transnational and international collaboration. 4) Localism and bottom-up approaches. 5) Complicated and complex methods.

Three important issues will be highlighted in this discussion about **the state** and theories of change. 1) The responsibilities of the state with regard to change. 2) Optimal relations between various actors – other states, inter-governmental organisations (IGOs), NGOs, etc. – and a given state. 3) Links between roles and relationships, and how changing relationships can modify roles. With regard to the state, three key tensions between development and human rights theories of change can be identified. The first is whether there is a development-human rights trade off, especially at the early stages of development. This tension relates to the classic debate about whether a state should sacrifice civil and political rights at the early stages of economic development. Second, while human rights organisations often have an adversarial relationship with governments, development actors, in part because they are much more dependent on governments as donors and in part because of the less politically contentious nature of their work, more usually work in

Operating across national boundaries

partnership with governments. Finally, the neo-liberal era of the shrinking, or 'hollowed out', state, raises the question of what role should NGOs play in service delivery. For example, should NGOs only deliver services when also building the capacity of the state to assume its responsibilities?

There are basically two views on the role of **law** in contributing to social change. One view is that the law leads, i.e. it may trigger, facilitate or speed up change; a second view is that the law follows change, i.e. it legally codifies and thus consolidates the change that has taken place. Under the former view the law is considered proactive, under the latter reactive. While it may be premature to draw any firm conclusions, it is clear that human rights law, more than any other branch of the law, can be seen as a potential lever for change. That potential has been explored in particular in strategic litigation. Empirically, it has become clear that the effectiveness of litigation in bringing about change needs to be contextualised, qualified and linked to broader policy provisions. Only when certain conditions are met, may human rights litigation have the direct and indirect impacts looked for.

Two main models for **transnational and international cooperation** are dominant, each with its own theory of change: 1) North-South partnerships, which continue to characterise much development work. 2) Transnational advocacy networks, which are an important point of reference in the human rights literature. The latter literature relates to theories of change in that it seeks to understand changes in state compliance with international norms, and suggest processes or pathways through which actors such as NGOs and IGOs can help facilitate this goal. By identifying methods beyond the purely adversarial, the transnational advocacy literature helps to build bridges between human rights and related fields such as development. In contrast the North-South partnership theory of change takes neither the state nor international norms as its point of departure, but rather tries to empower and build the capacity of local actors in the belief that this will enable change to be locally owned, legitimate and sustainable.

If transnational and international collaboration can be critiqued for being a top-down theory of change, more locally driven, **bottom-up alternatives** do exist. The main development modalities that focus on local context, power and politics prioritise participation, empowerment and citizenship, while an actor-oriented perspective serves a similar function within human rights. Perhaps the main area of tension between development and human rights in this context is the relative priority to be given to process versus outcomes criteria. Localism and bottom-up approaches champion not just a particular direction of change but also particular ways of working, which may take precedence over pre-conceived outcomes (such as the contents of national legislation or international treaties). As such, organisations and communities may define, prioritise, and champion rights that are not legally recognised.

between nations.

Much of the above discussion indicates the importance of **complicated and complex methods** in both development and human rights. Such methods are in part a function of history – and history depositing a layered archaeology from past political eras, priorities and cycles of donor funding. But such an approach is also an active choice in the present, and a statement that complex problems require complex interventions and solutions i.e. a rejection of simplistic linear, cause and effect, theories of change. Rogers (2008) makes a useful distinction between complicated and complex interventions. Complicated interventions have lots of parts (multiple components, multiple agencies, multiple causal strands). Complex interventions have uncertain and emergent outcomes (multidirectional causal relationships, 'tipping points', intractable problems). Using complicated and complex approaches has implications for the skills required to undertake development and human rights work and the strategies employed, but also raises difficult questions about prioritisation, sequencing, the relationship between different kinds of intervention, and appropriate divisions of labour between various actors or professional sectors.

Both development and human rights are characterised by diverse theories of change, and intersections between the two fields are adding to the complexity. The five entry-points to theories of change outlined above are not mutually exclusive – local struggles against oppression can resonate though transnational and international networks, for example – and indeed may be more powerful in combination, but neither can they all be embraced without contradiction. Some are focused and narrowly construed, others are more ambitious and wide-ranging. The entry-points raise questions about appropriate divisions of labour and relationships between the state and other actors; the role of law in bringing about broad-based social and policy change; the formation of optimal change alliances and networks; choices to be made with regard to top-down versus bottom-up as well as process- versus outcome-led approaches; and how organisations and sectors should prepare for a complicated and complex world. Despite their differences, theories of change in human rights and development will focus on broadly similar challenges: who to work with, how to legitimise the activities undertaken, the level of ambition, how to prioritise, etc. It is also clear that the overlaps between human rights and development are growing – raising a broader meta-question relating to the desirability of the growing overlap in philosophy and methodology in the social justice sector (often driven by human rights), and its implications for organisational identity and practice.

To conclude, this chapter argues that there are gains to be achieved by making implicit, partially formed theories of change in human rights work more explicit. By providing a roadmap to change, theories of change serve various goals: showing a causal pathway by specifying what is needed for goals to be achieved; articulating underlying assumptions which can be tested and measured; telling a story about how change happens that can be developed with and articulated to others; changing the way of thinking about an intervention from a focus on what is being done to the change that is sought; and facilitating cycles of learning. There is one main caveat to this argument: the value and contribution of theories of change will depend on *how* they are embraced and made explicit. Theories of change may shift human rights in the direction of top down, donor driven, technical, quantifiable objectives or they could prioritise bottom up approaches, context and local constituencies, challenges to power, and qualitative measures of change. For the latter to occur, human rights will need to not just embrace theories of change but also to transform them.

Bibliography

Aragón, A. and J. Macedo (2010) 'A "systemic theories of change" approach for purposeful capacity development', *IDS Bulletin* 41 (3), pp. 87–99.

Eyben, R., T. Kidder, J. Rowlands and A. Bronstein (2008) 'Thinking about change for development practice: a case study from Oxfam UK', *Development in Practice* 18 (2), pp. 201–12.

Gready, P. and W. Vandenhole (eds.) (2014) *Human Rights and Development in the New Millennium: Towards a Theory of Change* (London: Routledge).

Rogers, R. (2008) 'Using programme theory to evaluate complicated and complex aspects of Interventions', *Evaluation* 14 (1), pp. 29–48.

Vandenhole, W. and P. Gready (2014) 'Failures and successes of human rights-based approaches to development: towards a change perspective', *Nordic Journal of Human Rights* 32 (4), pp. 291–311.

8

(+ typical example)

Shifting sands: a paradigm change in the development discourse on women's human rights and empowerment

Catherine Klirodotakou

International human rights declarations, conventions and protocols such as the Universal Declaration of Human Rights (UDHR) and the Convention on the Elimination of All Forms of Discrimination against Women (CEDAW), are universally recognised as constituting the basis for demanding and achieving gender equality. They 'set a vision of a world where there is justice' (Cornwall 2015) and today it is widely acknowledged that the normative approach to development should be rights based, even if it's not the norm in practice. This discord is particularly evident in the women's rights development discourse. Securing women's empowerment has increasingly been dominating the international development agenda, but many consider the model being disseminated as *de-radicalised*, removed from its feminist activist roots and pursuing an apolitical ideology (Cornwall and Molyneux 2006). This in turn promotes and supports a very narrow definition of empowerment; one that does not seek wholesale substantive and transformative change for women and society, but seems to be content to work within and even embrace the existing socio-economic framework.

A blueprint for securing rights and empowerment

2015 marks the 20th anniversary of the adoption of the Beijing Declaration and Platform for Action (BPfA). It was and remains a bold and progressive blueprint, drafted and agreed by 189 governments, to advance women's rights and empowerment globally. It ushered in an era of important global pacts such as the United Nations Security Council Resolution 1325 (2000), which recognised the impact of conflict on women, and their central role in building peace. However, despite this progress, the world has changed significantly since the adoption of the BPfA; conflict, extremism, climate change, natural disasters and the global financial crisis, to name but a few, have all contributed to a climate in which there are growing attempts to water down previously agreed international obligations and commitments. Perversely, this threat comes at a time when women's *empowerment* has never been more popular with governments, donors and civil society organisations alike. The prevailing rhetoric is that women's human rights, women's empowerment and gender equality are central to the international development agenda.

New actors but a shrinking space

Women – and girls in particular – seem to be the panacea to all our development woes. Get more women into the workplace and your economy will be thriving; educate girls and the whole community prospers; turn women into politicians and peace and security will prevail. One would consider this a victory: women's rights are finally on the agenda like never before, but there is something not quite right with this picture. We are witnessing an era where the agents of this change are not women themselves and women's rights organisations, but increasingly mainstream international development agencies and multilateral and bilateral development institutions. The women's rights movement – which was key to raising consciousness and building momentum for gender equality in the past – is not driving this process. Many may consider that this is how it should be: women's human rights and gender equality should not be the domain of the few but be embraced, supported and mainstreamed. But this mainstreaming of the women's human rights and gender equality is going hand in hand with a fundamental shift in what is considered and practiced as empowerment; both as a goal in itself and as a process.

Critics of this agenda view efforts to secure women's human rights and empower women as increasingly being co-opted into an instrumentalist, apolitical, results-based, cause and effect paradigm. In short, securing women's rights becomes a means to tackle poverty under a neoliberal economic model. In this scenario violence and discrimination against women become bitesize tangible dilemmas, which are compartmentalised and tackled in time-bound projects. Andrea Cornwall (2007) has coined this type of piecemeal approach to development as *empowerment lite* – the focus is on numbers, alleviating the symptoms of poverty and oppression, but not addressing the power imbalance nor contributing to any meaningful transformative empowerment for women. A form of *empowerment lite* in action can be seen in the Millennium Development Goal 3 (MDG3),[1] which focussed on a narrow definition of empowerment; one based on education, employment and political participation and did little to

1   The Millennium Development Goals are the eight international development goals to be achieved by 2015, that were established following the Millennium Summit of the United Nations in 2000, following the adoption of the United Nations Millennium Declaration. MDG3 is to 'promote gender equality and empower women'.

consider the multi-dimensional aspect of inequality, how to address patriarchy, or pursue transformative forms of women's agency (Kabeer 2005).

Challenging patriarchy, transforming societies

Reclaiming the discourse on empowerment as a way to challenge patriarchy, transform the structures and institutions that reinforce and perpetuate discrimination and inequality, and enable women to gain access to, and control of, resources (Batliwala 1994) is one of the biggest challenges we face as women's rights activists and practitioners. Having frameworks to call States and other duty bearers to account is an important platform that underpins the work of women's rights organisations. The lack of commitment towards substantive progress on achieving women's human rights, however, is impeding efforts in securing long-term transformational changes in the lives of women and girls. The increasing instrumentalist focus on women as a means to an end and the overwhelming focus to articulate poverty and inequality as one-dimensional cause and effect, reflects a de-politicisation of women's empowerment and gender equality. Increasingly women's rights organisations are facing the dilemma of either adapting to this paradigmatic shift or potentially facing extinction.

The de-politicisation of securing women's rights

In this context it has become increasingly hard to articulate women's inequality and discrimination as manifestations of power over access to and control of resources. Legal reform alone is not enough to tackle social norms, attitudes and practices that perpetuate women's subordination; projects that do not take a holistic approach to addressing violence, discrimination and inequality cannot bring about substantive changes in securing women's rights. For instance, women's rights organisations in Ghana such as the Gender Studies and Human Rights Documentation Centre and Women in Law and Development in Africa, recognise that quotas alone will not get more women into politics, and that there is a need to work at different levels from the personal to the international. Their approach looks at creating women only or safe spaces for women, to gain confidence, skills and knowledge, before they even start to consider taking on leadership positions. Simultaneously they recognise the need to create an enabling environment which accepts and supports women's participation and they do that by engaging with different actors such as traditional leaders, community members, local authorities, the media and politicians. What these organisations inherently understand is that unless they tackle structural inequality and focus on women's voice and agency, then any gains will be short lived and will not contribute to a transformation of society.

A recent study has reaffirmed the catalytic role that women's rights organisations play in such interventions. The four-decade research programme which looked at 70 countries found that the mobilisation of women's organisations and movements is more important for combating violence against women than the wealth of nations, left-wing political parties, or the number of women politicians (Htun and Weldon 2012). Yet despite such evidence there are numerous examples of the disparity between rhetoric and practice. In Sierra Leone a local women's rights organisation lost vital funding from an international NGO when they chose to support a mainstream civil society organisation instead, to deliver work on addressing violence against women and girls (VAWG). Two years later that same INGO, which considers women's rights one of its main areas of work, profiled their ex-partner in a report about the increasing marginalisation of women's rights organisations.

One Zimbabwean women's rights organisation – recognised internationally for its efforts to address women's civil and political participation – described how they are increasingly being forced into carrying out work that takes a power and even gender neutral approach to tackling women's exclusion. They see the personal transformation element of their approach as key, but donors seem not to. Building a strong sense of self and agency in women appears not to be easily measurable and not immediately clear as to how it contributes to good governance. Instead their work has to be framed in demanding provision of basic social services and livelihood skills development. The rhetoric appears to be apolitical; poverty and exclusion are presented as a product of women not being economically empowered, thus all women need is access to resources and the rest will follow – seemingly a win-win for development and for women. But we need to be questioning whether these are mutually reinforcing. Despite evidence pointing to the need to collectively address empowerment, equality and rights, there are numerous examples of empowerment initiatives that circumvent the other two. Take Water, Sanitation and Hygiene (WASH) programmes for instance: in recent years they have been increasingly presented as a means to reduce VAWG. Resources are being poured into this type of work, despite evidence pointing to the fact that there is no tangible reduction in VAWG (Fulu, Kerr-Wilson, and Lang 2014).

2015 and beyond

In the Sustainable Development Goals, which will replace the MDGs in 2016, we have an opportunity to try to redress the situation and bring *power* back into empowerment work. A strong commitment to human rights is key but within a framework that seeks transformation and is robust enough to address the deep rooted and persistent structural gender inequalities that exist. Women's rights organisations need to be in the driving seat and the development agenda must meet the actual needs and concerns of women at the local level. It has to recognise that in today's globalised world there are new actors, such as transnational corporations, financial institutions and private foundations, that we need to be demanding accountability from and it has to foster women's collective action to monitor and remedy the shifting sands of the rights and development discourse. This means reclaiming Batliwala's (1994) notion of empowerment of challenging patriarchy, transforming structures and institutions and enabling women to gain access to, and control of, resources.

Bibliography

Batliwala, S. (1994) 'The meaning of women's empowerment: new concepts from action', in G. Sen, A. Germain and L. C. Chen (eds.), *Population Policies Reconsidered: Health, Empowerment and Rights* (Cambridge: Harvard University Press).

Cornwall, A. and M. Molyneux (2006) 'The politics of rights: dilemmas for feminist praxis', *Third World Quarterly* 27 (7), pp. 1175–91.

Cornwall, A. (2007) 'Pathways of women's empowerment', in *50.50 Inclusive Democracy* (30 July 2007), available at https://www.opendemocracy.net/article/pathways_of_womens_empowerment (accessed 10 Sept. 2015).

— (2015) 'Why gender equality by numbers will never measure up', *The Guardian* (26 March 2015), available at http://www.theguardian.com/global-development/2015/mar/26/why-gender-equality-by-numbers-never-measure-up-mdg3–stereotypes (accessed 10 Sept. 2015).

Fulu, E., A. Kerr-Wilson and J. Lang (2014) 'What works to prevent violence against women and girls? Evidence review of interventions to prevent violence against women and girls', in *DFID Violence against women and girls guidance notes* (30 July 2014), available at https://www.gov.uk/government/publications/what-works-in-preventing-violence-against-women-and-girls-review-of-the-evidence-from-the-programme (accessed 10 Sept. 2015).

Htun, M. and L. Weldon (2012) 'The civic origins of progressive policy change: combating violence against women in global perspective, 1975–2005', *American Political Science Review* 106 (3), pp. 548–69.

Kabeer, N. (2005) 'Gender equality and women's empowerment: a critical analysis of the third millennium development goal 1', *Gender & Development* 13 (1), pp. 13–24.

9

The role of human rights in diversity management and conflict prevention[1]

Sally Holt

Diversity along ethnic, cultural, religious and linguistic lines exists as a matter of fact within all our societies as a result of migration of people across political boundaries or the changing of those boundaries themselves. Such cultural diversity[2] is not a new phenomenon. This chapter argues that States should take active steps to effectively manage the diversity within their jurisdiction and sets out a 'human rights-informed' approach for doing so. It examines the different roles that international human rights law (IHRL) can play in managing diversity, while also acknowledging its limitations. It aims to show how the approach complements and builds on rights-based approaches by acknowledging the relevance and potential of other normative frameworks and principles in addition to those of human rights in processes of diversity management.

The argument for diversity management

Regardless of the level of a country's development, the nature of its political system or whether it is essentially peaceful or on the brink of (or in the midst of) violent conflict, diversity requires proactive management in policy, legislation and practice for both principled and pragmatic reasons. In democratic societies founded on majority rule, the culture of the majority (or otherwise dominant group) tends to enjoy privileged status within the State whether due to formal/

---

1 This chapter draws on the following sources: S. Holt and Z. Machnyikova (2013) 'Culture for Shared Societies', in M. Fitzduff (ed.), *Public Policies in Shared Societies: A Comparative Approach* (New York: Palgrave), pp. 167–214; and S. Holt 'Managing Diversity: Culture', *Conflict Prevention Handbook Series*, No. 7, Initiative on Quiet Diplomacy, forthcoming 2015.
2 The term 'cultural diversity' is used here to denote the existence within a population of people from a variety or multiformity of ethnic, cultural, religious or linguistic backgrounds.

legal status or simply as matter of fact. Those in a non-dominant position are left at a disadvantage. Minority groups may be (or feel) marginalised, discriminated against or otherwise face challenges and obstacles relating both to aspects of maintaining, developing, expressing and transmitting their distinct cultural identities in public and private, and with regard to their full participation in the political, social and economic life of the State. In this regard, barriers to accessing public services and other resources or opportunities on an equitable basis are common.

Unequal societies that leave some groups marginalised and alienated are not only unjustifiable from a rights perspective, they are also inefficient and damaging for society as a whole because they exclude the talents, resources and beneficial contributions of significant sections of the population. Inequality also potentially creates resentments and tensions, both in terms of communities' relationships with State authorities and/or between different groups within society. Manifestations of frustration by the excluded can provoke or increase chauvinism and hostility from the wider society, which may in turn exacerbate divisions and tensions and, in some cases, escalate into violence. Diversity is by no means inevitably a source of conflict, but such tensions are easily exploited for political ends, with fears or prejudices amongst different groups whipped up by those intent on engendering conflict for their own gain. In many cases cultural identity has a role in violent conflict, not as a root cause, but as a driver for political mobilisation to wrest or maintain a hold on power. Once violence has started more grievances accrue on both sides and the conflict may continue even after initial grievances have been remedied. It is therefore essential to address contentious issues before tensions erupt into violence. It is noteworthy that the absence of overt tensions or violent conflict does not necessarily signal successful management of cultural diversity. A pattern of peaceful enforced domination of one group by another is particularly prone to breakdown.

Obstacles and challenges

Despite increasing recognition of cultural diversity as a feature of all societies, in many countries acceptance of this fact has yet to translate into concrete policies and practices that effectively accommodate diversity. The first step to effective policy lies in official recognition of the existence of diversity and of the rights, interests and aspirations of different groups. In practice, many States seek to restrict the enjoyment of universal human rights, and particularly minority rights, to selected communities. Even where official recognition is in place, the implementation of effective policies can be impeded by a lack of political will related to common reasons for resistance to change, including: failure to understand the need for or the potential benefits of change; fear of the unknown; adherence to beliefs and misconceptions about the threat to society posed by diversity; and pressure from the media and popular opinion based on similar fears and misconceptions.

Another major challenge, particularly in States transitioning from authoritarian regimes, is simply the lack of knowledge or experience of the frameworks, mechanisms and options available for successful diversity management. In the experience of the OSCE High Commissioner on National Minorities (HCNM) (a regional mechanism dedicated to resolving minority-related tensions within and between States) policy and law-makers in newly independent States of the former Soviet Union and across Central and Eastern Europe were often quite open to receiving specific guidance to help them develop effective responses to diversity-related tensions within their jurisdictions in line with their international commitments.[3]

A human rights-informed approach[4]

A human rights-informed approach recognises that, while societies and situations may differ, precluding universal policy prescriptions or 'recipes', lessons can nevertheless be drawn from an examination of the comparative practice of States in implementing their obligations under IHRL and building peaceful cohesive societies. Examples of 'effective practice' (i.e. generally or specifically successful practices proven to work in real situations) include: constitutional guarantees of human rights, including minority rights; devolution or other territorial arrangements for self-governance; equitable State investment, expenditure and resource allocation; positive measures, including affirmative action policies, as well as special measures to support and promote various different cultures; and policies and measures aimed at improving relations between different cultural communities. Lessons can also be gleaned from examples of bad or 'ineffective' practice, including the unintended consequences of exclusionary or 'culturally blind' laws and policies.

Given the diversity of practice between (and sometimes within) States, IHRL can provide a useful framework for understanding and managing diversity and for preventing violent conflict in several ways:

3   The HCNM provides tailored guidance to individual States. The office has also overseen the development of a series of thematic recommendations and guidelines on recurrent issues arising in the course of the HCNM's engagement, including matters of language, education, effective participation in public life, policing and inter-State relations. The full set of thematic recommendations is available at OSCE, *Thematic Recommendations and Guidelines*, available at http://www.osce. org/hcnm/66209 (accessed 18 Sept. 2015).

4   The 'human-rights informed approach' was initially conceived and implemented in practice under the first OSCE High Commissioner on National Minorities, Max van der Stoel. It was further developed and promoted in other regions of the world by the *Initiative on Quiet Diplomacy* (http://www.iqdiplomacy.org/) under the leadership of Prof. John Packer, former Director of the Office of the OSCE HCNM.

1. In the *identification of human rights violations* that underlie tensions and conflict. Crucially, IHRL prohibits discrimination based on race, religion, language or ethnicity, among other grounds, and it confers specific rights on persons belonging to minorities and indigenous peoples who are often disadvantaged by virtue of their cultural identity. Where discrimination, exclusion, or marginalisation of certain communities or groups is a source of grievance against the State and of inter-community tensions it is essential that policy-makers are able to identify and effectively address sources of injustice, including all forms of discrimination where they exist.[5]

2. As a *source of leverage* for both international and national actors (including those whose rights have been violated) in holding States to account for failing to live up to their obligations under IHRL and pressing for measures that will prevent or mitigate conflict. These may relate to the need for effective remedy for individual violations, as well as structural changes to legislation, policy and practice to prevent recurrence of such violations in future.

3. As a *principled framework* for analysing situations and developing appropriate responses. IHRL provides a set of underlying principles to be adhered to. Key in this regard are the principles of non-discrimination and equality, and of participation. Non-discrimination and equality includes States' obligations to take 'special measures' to address past discrimination (often referred to as 'affirmative action') and to ensure equality in fact for members of communities who are in a (permanently) disadvantaged position by virtue of their group identity. Principles of participation including the management of one's own or the group's cultural affairs are also fundamental to diversity management. This implies a degree of self-governance that can be realised through various arrangements for the community concerned. At the same time, ensuring equal opportunities for effective participation in all relevant decision-making processes of the State is essential in building peaceful cohesive societies in which everyone has a stake. To this end, measures for the recognition, protection and promotion of distinct cultural identities must be complemented by measures for the inclusion of communities within society as a whole, including via political and economic opportunities and social relations. The promotion of mutual respect, understanding and tolerance between communities, particularly in the fields of culture, education and the media — as enshrined in human rights (including minority rights) standards — are also essential to this process.

5   For detailed guidance on identifying and addressing discrimination see Hollo (2011).

In addition to setting out a broad principled framework, IHRL provides guidance in determining what is possible and permissible when developing policy, legal and institutional approaches to diversity management. It sets parameters in terms of legitimate limitations on individual rights and freedoms and provides a methodology for mediating between competing interests or claims where the rights of one individual or community clash with the rights of others or with the wider public interest. This can entail a careful balancing act for which the jurisprudence of universal and regional human rights oversight bodies provides specific guidance, including factors for consideration, in assessing whether a restriction on an individual right related to cultural expression has a legitimate aim (i.e. it is in the public interest and/or to protect the rights of others) and is proportional to that aim (i.e. is the least restrictive for achieving the required result). For example, where a woman's right to express her culture or religion by covering her head or face in public is balanced against national security interests in ensuring images on identity documents allow easy identification of individuals. Similarly, rights of indigenous peoples to access traditional lands, sites or monuments of cultural or religious significance to them may conflict with the public interest in economic development that (potentially) takes place on the same land.[6]

A human rights-informed approach recognises that in addition to the normative framework of human rights, principles of *good governance* can be instrumental in identifying potential sources of tension relating to cultural diversity and devising appropriate responses to effectively manage them. Good governance signifies that governing institutions are committed to creating comparable conditions and equal opportunities for all to pursue their development and fulfil their aspirations.[7] In some cases, there may not exist a human right to State support for a certain aspect of cultural life, but principles of good governance (and experience) indicate that such situations should nevertheless be addressed. They also provide a useful guide for how to do so. For example, access to higher education in a minority language has been a contentious issue in a number of States. There is no provision under IHRL that guarantees State-funded tertiary minority language education, but bilingual and multi-lingual initiatives that respond to communities' demands for mother-tongue education, while also ensuring equal access to education in

---

6   For guidance in analysing and addressing a range of problematic situations relating to cultural diversity using a human rights framework see Holt and Machnyikova (2013), Table 8.1.

7   For an overview of the relationships between good governance and human rights see United Nations Office of the High Commissioner for Human Rights, *Good Governance and Human Rights,* available at http://www.ohchr.org/EN/Issues/Development/GoodGovernance/Pages/GoodGovernanceIndex.aspx (accessed 18 Sept. 2015).

the State languages (and international languages) have helped to defuse tense situations, e.g. in the Balkans.[8]

A human rights-informed approach also recognises the *limitations of a human rights framework* in reconciling differences around culture. Indeed, it can often be the claim or realisation of a right — or the way that right is expressed — that becomes a source of hostility or resentment between individuals or groups of different cultural backgrounds. For example, one community's exercise of their right to practice their religion by establishing a place of prayer can represent a symbolic marking of public space that provokes unease in others, particularly where a fear of the unfamiliar or a sense of vulnerability in terms of their own identity already exists. Local level disputes can easily become politicised, both feeding into and influenced by wider debates around the State's approaches (existing or desired) to the management of cultural difference. In such cases, a range of diplomatic means are available for managing tensions, including through techniques and mechanisms for dialogue and mediation, with a view to achieving outcomes acceptable to all parties.[9]

The approach also respects *other legal frameworks* insofar as these are compatible with IHRL. In addition to human rights, humanitarian and refugee law and standards pertaining specifically to internally displaced person (IDPs), as well as religious, cultural and economic norms (among others) can all play a role in diversity management.

Finally, the approach recognises that in some contexts the *use of human rights language* can be counter-productive. This can be the case where concepts of human rights are unfamiliar and/or are regarded by large sections of the population as 'a Western imposition' irrelevant to the local culture.[10] For example, ongoing work with women MPs in Tunisia exploring ways to more effectively support their participation in politics and wider peacebuilding has highlighted the challenges of using human rights discourses where a secular (human rights) vs. religious divide permeates politics and society. In this case it has been possible to engage meaningfully with women from different positions and backgrounds, sometimes using human rights language (e.g. with civil society activists who frame their work in these terms), but also by engaging Islamic feminist discourses exploring more progressive interpretations of Islam,[11] as well as practical methodologies for personal empowerment rooted

---

8   For recent development in Serbia, for example, see OSCE, *OSCE High Commissioner on National Minorities focuses on education during visit to Serbia* (2 September 2014), available at http://www.osce.org/hcnm/123111 (accessed 18 Sept. 2015).

9   For guidance in this respect, see Collins and Packer (2006).

10 On the need for more contextualised approaches to promoting women's rights see, for example, British and Irish Agencies Afghanistan Group (2014).

11 Although the term 'Islamic feminism' is also contentious in the Tunisian context.

in religious and cultural norms prevalent in Muslim-majority societies in the region.[12]

Conclusion

A 'human rights-informed' approach to managing diversity and preventing conflict provides a structure within which advocates of different positions may find a common basis for discussion. It provides both a principled framework and a range of practical options and benchmarks for consideration in identifying and developing policy, legislative and institutional responses that are context-sensitive and appropriate. In doing so it draws on examples of individual States' practice in effectively managing diversity in line with their obligations under IHRL. The approach in no way diminishes or undermines rights-based approaches. Rather, it aims to maximise their potential to practically assist policy-makers and conflict prevention actors in understanding and responding to the challenges facing them in ways that are both conflict-sensitive and in conformity with international law. In also recognising the limitations of using human rights language in some contexts, a human rights-informed approach supports the possibility (and often probability) of effecting change that respects and promotes human rights in fact, but without insisting upon explicit reference to IHRL.

Bibliography

British and Irish Agencies Afghanistan Group (2014) *Getting it right: Examining Gender Programming in Afghanistan*, conference report, October 2014, available at http://www.baag.org.uk/sites/www.baag. org.uk/files/resources/attachments/Getting%20it%20Right%202014_ FINAL.pdf (accessed 18 Sept. 2015).

Collins, C. and J. Packer (2006) 'Options and Techniques of quiet diplomacy', *Conflict Prevention Handbook Series*, No.1, Initiative on Quiet Diplomacy, available at http://library.nhrc.or.th/ulib/document/Fulltext/ F05872.pdf (accessed 18 Sept. 2015).

Hollo, L. (2011) 'Discrimination and conflict prevention', *Conflict Prevention Handbook Series*, No.2, Initiative on Quiet Diplomacy, available at http:// www.iqdiplomacy.org/images/stories/handbook/pdf/discrimination_ iqd2_02.pdf

Holt, S. 'Managing diversity: culture', *Conflict Prevention Handbook Series*, No. 7, Initiative on Quiet Diplomacy, forthcoming 2015.

---

12 For more on this methodology, see 'Success in a Changing World', developed by the International Forum for Islamic Dialogue, http://www.ifid.org.uk.

Holt, S. and Z. Machnyikova (2013) 'Culture for shared societies', in M. Fitzduff (ed.), *Public Policies in Shared Societies: A Comparative Approach* (New York: Palgrave), pp. 167–214.

10

Why tax is a human rights issue: empowering communities living in poverty to hold governments to account for public services

Bridget Burrows[1]

Tax pays for public services

Sitting on the floor the villagers are drawing a map of their area. They're marking all the essential services they use, including those that are provided by the government and those that are private. The community map they're creating has little on it. There is no public school, nor public health clinic. The water borehole they use was built by an NGO. As the women and men discuss, the sense of the government as a provider of public services is almost non-existent. The access to the local government with the power to make decisions is a district official, in the nearest district town, which is a long distance.

1   All views in this article are the author's own and not those of ActionAid.

For many decades the centre of the conversation between communities such as this one in Uganda, civil society and governments around the world has been that the state needs to give money to build a classroom, and pay the teachers' wages, and build a road, for this village. For each interest group, the conversation has been that the government needs to give more money to particular sectors, often competing, such as education, health, agriculture, roads, and security.

A lot of important work has been done by civil society and activists, both to increase national budget allocations to public services, and to ensure via participatory community budget tracking that the money is well-spent on things that help communities living in poverty, and not lost on corruption. This article is about an important third part of the triangle: not how money is allocated, or how money is spent, but how money is raised. It is about the slippery heart of economic, social and cultural rights: that the government must progressively realise them according to 'maximum available resources' (International Covenant on Economic, Social and Cultural Rights, Article 2.1). Fundamentally, it is about when governments point to empty budgets, about being able to point to reforms in fiscal policy that could provide fairer resources, and about the necessity and challenges of supporting communities living in poverty to be part of this to ensure it is well spent on public services that have a huge impact on people's rights.

At the time of writing, the world is getting ready to pat itself on the back for a new round of global anti-poverty targets, the Sustainable Development Goals. While the goals are successful as a way of building globally agreed indicators on the progressive realisation of economic, social, and cultural rights, one question becomes increasingly pertinent: to make them a reality, where will the money come from?

As development aid budgets come under pressure, two new watchwords are emerging in financing for development conversations, both in opposition to each other, and representing a wider trend: domestic resource mobilisation and private finance. For instance, at the 2014 Global Partnership for Education (GPE) funding replenishment conference, developing countries pledged USD 26 billion to spending on education, committing to help fund it by increasing their domestic resource mobilisation. This was ten times more than the USD 2.1 billion pledged by donors, and represents a dramatic shift of focus for development financing.

The money pledged by developing country governments is basically coming from national taxation. Currently, according to the World Bank, 'tax revenues accounted for 10–14 per cent of GDP in low-income countries in 2009 and just under 20 per cent of GDP in middle-income countries. This compares to about 33 per cent in OECD countries, rising above 40 per cent in some European countries' (ActionAid 2015, 7).

A 2014 Education for All Global Monitoring Report looked at increasing tax revenues to bridge the education financing gap. They showed that if governments in 67 low and middle income countries modestly increased their tax-raising efforts and devoted a fifth of their budget to education, they could raise an additional US 153 billion for education spending in 2015, increasing the average share of GDP spent on education from 3 per cent to 6 per cent by 2015 (Education for All Global Monitoring Report 2014, 1).

One study gives a glimpse of the potential impact of a government's revenue raising on the achievement of the previous set of goals, the Millennium Development Goals (MDGs) (Waris and Matti Kohonen 2011). The research found that in almost all cases, the more tax a country collected in relation to its GDP, the better their realisation of the MDGs. Whether it was the number of children dying before their fifth birthday, or the number of teenage girls giving birth, or the number of young people that can read and write, the more tax a government collected, the better the development results. This could of course be a correlation, rather than a cause (governments that are organising better to collect tax also may be organising better to achieve the MDGs), but it is likely that some of this is because more money is also being spent on essential public services that help realise the MDGs. Clearly more research is needed.

Lost tax revenue

Unfortunately, many developing countries have fairly regressive tax systems that depend too much on indirect consumer taxes as a way of increasing the tax

take, adding pennies to every purchase made by a poor household. This means that it is national citizens, including people living in poverty, who are behind a significant part of the money that is spent to finance essential public services. This increases the case for national citizens, including those living in poverty, to hold national governments to account for delivering on rights.

A large potential contributor to the tax system is not being captured. Over the last two decades, foreign investment has grown considerably as a share of the economy of low-income countries, from around 7 per cent in the 1990s to over 20 per cent in 2010, but tellingly, corporate tax paid in the same period has meandered along in a dishearteningly flat line (ActionAid 2015, 9). In short, countries' budgets are not benefiting much from all this investment.

One of the reasons is that governments are simply giving the tax money away. An ActionAid International and Tax Justice Network-Africa study (2012) found that in 2009/10, the Government of Uganda gave multinational companies USD 272 million in exemptions on their tax bill. To put this in perspective, it is enough money at the time to have doubled the health budget overnight. Alternatively, with average teacher wages at about USD 1,800 a year, it could have paid for 150,000 extra teachers a year, or it could have built around 10,500 extra classroom blocks. Remembering our village without a public school or health clinic, the amount of tax money being given away could be transformational.

Tax can be seen as a technical or economic issue but ActionAid's focus is on justice – on how big companies not paying their fair share of tax and governments not spending it on public services negatively impacts communities living in poverty, financing for development, and the fulfillment of human rights. Globally, ActionAid revealed that USD 138 billion is lost to corporate income tax breaks given by poor countries to multinationals every year (ActionAid 2013). The amounts are so large, they are enough to school all 57 million children who currently don't go to primary school, provide the agricultural investment (USD 42.7 billion) needed to achieve a world free from hunger, and meet international goals to reduce ill health more than twice over (USD 58.9 billion). This only represents the tax money that governments are *choosing* to give away, and not what multinational companies are *avoiding* through exploiting loopholes in weak tax laws. When we think about maximum available resources for the Millennium Development Goals, it becomes clear the impact a few simple reforms to create more progressive tax systems could have on financing for development. Ironically, the evidence shows that these tax giveaways have very little impact on foreign investment in poor countries, and that indeed, what foreign investors actually want is access to consumer markets, infrastructure and educated workforces – the very things created by tax-funded development.

Progressive tax, progressively spent

This is part of a much bigger global trend, with increasing global inequality of private power and wealth negatively impacting on the ability of governments to meet their obligations to fulfill economic and social rights. The problem is compounded as the less that governments progressively raise and spend tax, the more public services decline, and the more appetite it creates for private actors to step into the market and provide privatised essential services. The evidence in the education sector in developing countries supported by the Privatisation in Education Research Initiative (PERI) shows that these privatised services are negatively impacting the accessibility of education rights for all children and particularly for girls. When low income parents have to pay to access basic services they prefer to send boys.

A fair tax system not only raises revenue for human rights. It can also redistribute wealth, reducing inequality and the gap between rich and poor within countries and between countries. Taxes are the most reliable and sustainable source of government revenue, compared to overseas aid, loans or private funding. A fair tax system can increase representation and accountability, of the state to citizens, encouraging better governance and more independent and responsive policy-making.

For ActionAid tax justice is: governments having the ability to raise enough tax to provide quality public services; governments raising and spending tax transparently, progressively, and accountably to citizens; the international community helping create transparent and fair global tax rules which help governments to access all relevant information and establish fair national tax systems; and global companies making fair tax payments where business is transacted, resources are extracted, and profits are made.

Communities holding governments to account for public services

Following our human rights-based approach, ActionAid's campaign signature is of community-led campaigning, particularly by women and marginalised people, in defence of their rights. But if you're from that village in Uganda that we started in, with little access to government and few multinational companies or their products in sight, what does all this mean to you?

Many people do not even know that they are a taxpayer through consumer taxes, and that they have a right to demand a fairer tax system, or accountability for what the government does with the money. Indeed, public services are often seen as a gift from government, rather than a right or even a service. The communities living in poverty that ActionAid works with experience tax injustice directly in two ways. Firstly, through unfair local taxation, such as high consumer taxes on essential goods, and multiple taxation where different branches of government are taxing the same thing many times. Secondly, through the lack of essential public services, such as schools and hospitals.

Women, who often fill the gap where quality public services don't exist through providing unpaid care work looking after the sick, the elderly and the young, pay not only tax, but also pay with their bodies and time, impacting on their ability to seek employment or study.

It is from these starting points that ActionAid seeks to encourage community involvement in building progressive taxation systems. ActionAid recently developed a toolkit of participatory exercises to facilitate discussions in community groups on the relationship of tax to their lives and their rights. Each exercise goes through a few key ideas. One exercise asks community members to play characters, such as a woman farmer, a teacher, a national business, a foreign chief executive, and a tax collector, and then distributing and collecting pebbles to each character asking the group to create a scenario that is most 'fair.' When asked this question, they do the same as most of the world, which is to keep some people richer, and some people poorer, but distribute the pebbles far more evenly, creating greater equality.

ActionAid Uganda and local and national partners working with women farmers recently had a success on reducing unfair local taxation. In 2014, looking for more money, the Government of Uganda proposed to remove a tax exemption on basic farming goods, such as hoes and fertiliser. Analysing the budget, national civil society spotted the negative implications for millions of farmers, particularly poor women farmers, around the country.

They mobilised hundreds of thousands of women small-holder farmers to sign a petition to keep the tax exemption for basic farming items. The petition proposed that if the government needed money it should consider removing tax exemptions from large multinational companies instead. The petition and demonstrations were a success, and the government backed down. This success for the women farmers to assert themselves over tax and budget issues with local and national government opens a door to continuing to work on tax justice issues with them.

On the issue of lack of public services, one example comes from how ActionAid works with students, parents and teachers to carry out participatory rights-based assessments on the extent to which schools are delivering on ten key education rights, creating citizens' reports. The community then advocate with school management committees and district officials to create rights-based school improvement plans, claiming their rights and deepening local accountability. The plans, however, such as building separate toilet blocks that help girls to keep coming to school throughout the month, have a cost, and the fulfillment of rights can fall down at this stage.

ActionAid is exploring new work to link this evidence from communities seeking better schools to national and international level campaigning to finance education through tax justice. The work will start with ActionAid Malawi, Tanzania, Mozambique and Nepal and nine civil society partners, seeking to bring together teachers' unions, national education, budget tracking, and tax justice networks, to hold governments to account for progressive national tax reforms that will lead to increased local spending on public education.

However, for the villagers in Uganda who want a free quality education for their children, the tax justice journey is a long one. It assumes that if the government is convinced to change tax policy, that the money will be allocated to education, and that the money will reach local government and be well-spent. For women and men struggling for each day's bread, to stop and take action on such issues is a generous use of time. The lifetime of a campaign to achieve this may be longer than their children's education.

One of the challenges for ActionAid is to remain aware and cautious of ActionAid's own relative size and wealth, and that our efforts neither instrumentalise the communities living in poverty that we work with, or remove space from local and national allies. For ActionAid's human rights-based approach to truly empower and walk alongside communities living in poverty to demand their rights, we hope to support stronger local to international links to challenge the power and wealth structures at every level that impact on local provision of rights and to hold governments to account for quality public services over time. Our work with communities for tax justice for quality public services is only just starting.

[All photos courtesy of ActionAid]

Bibliography

ActionAid International (2013) *Give us a break: How big companies are getting tax free deals*, available at http://www.actionaid.org/sites/files/actionaid/give_us_a_break_-_how_big_companies_are_getting_tax-free_deals_2.pdf (accessed 16 Sept. 2015).

— (2015) *Levelling Up: Ensuring a fairer share of corporate tax for developing countries*, available at http://www.actionaid.org.uk/sites/default/files/publications/levelling_up_final.pdf (accessed 16 Sept. 2015).

ActionAid International and Tax Justice Network-Africa (2012) *Tax competition in East Africa: A race to the bottom? Tax incentives and revenue losses in Uganda*, available at http://www.actionaid.org/sites/files/actionaid/uganda_report1.pdf (accessed 16 Sept. 2015).

Education for All Global Monitoring Report (2014) *Policy Paper 12: Increasing tax revenues to bridge the education financing gap*, UNESCO, available at http://unesdoc.unesco.org/images/0022/002270/227092E.pdf (accessed 16 Sept. 2015).

Privatisation in Education Research Initiative, *PERI Research*, [website] http://www.periglobal.org/page/peri-research (Accessed 16 Sept. 2015).

Waris, A. and M. Kohonen (2011) *Linking Taxation to the Realisation of the Millenium Development Goals in Africa*, available at http://eadi.org/gc2011/waris-109.pdf (accessed 16 Sept. 2015).

11

Technical cooperation in the field of human rights

Farid Hamdan

This chapter highlights the contribution of the academic teaching which I have received at the University of London within the MA in Understanding and Securing of Human Rights in 2002–3. The course content and its themes have contributed to strengthening my knowledge and skills for the human rights field, which have enabled me to have better opportunities to contribute to human rights protection and promotion. Throughout the last years, I have worked extensively to transfer the knowledge gained into projects and practical programmes in the field of human rights, namely, capacity building through Technical Cooperation Programmes (TCPs).[1] In this chapter, I will use three examples to show the contribution of TCPs in building knowledge and skills to promote and protect human rights. The first example will focus on TCPs during conflict and insecurity; the second will show building skills during transition; and the third will show the country specific programme during stability.

Building capacities of rights holders and duty bearers during armed conflict

Hawa and Ezz Eldeen were among others from Internally Displaced Persons who were trained on training-of-trainers for local communities. As a result of a series of training programmes, they were able to know their rights and the rights of others. They were also skilled on how to defend themselves and other victims during armed conflict. They have become able to understand and use human rights related terms. They have also become able to provide victims with advice, especially women victims.

---

1 Technical Cooperation refers to the United Nations advisory service and assistance to Governments in the field of human rights. See UN Office of the High Commissioner for Human Rights, *Fact sheet No.3 (Rev.1), Advisory Service and Technical Cooperation in the Field of Human Rights*, Geneva: United Nations (1996). Available at http://www.ohchr.org/Documents/Publications/FactSheet3Rev.1en. pdf (accessed 17 Sept. 2015).

TCPs in conflict areas do not focus only on empowering victims but have also targeted duty bearers and placed both groups on its programme to protect human rights. At the same time, TCPs have targeted duty bearers from prison administrations, attorney generals and prosecutors, judges, and police investigators to promote awareness on the application of international human rights law. They also created forums for dialogue to find the best ways to improve the human rights situation in areas that have witnessed conflicts and human rights violations.

Important activities have been carried out in areas living in conflict and TCPs have had a positive impact on enhancing the role of victims in protecting themselves, albeit without improving the human rights situation or putting an end to the conflict. Such activities are varied, including:

- Organising training and awareness raising workshops on issues related to gender-based violence during the armed conflicts;
- Developing special training programmes to improve native administrations' capacities to respect gender and women's rights by promoting the concepts of equality and non-discrimination;
- Organising training programmes for governmental institutions, officials, prosecutors and judges on their role to respect human rights.

Implementing capacity building activities during armed conflict is not an easy task for many reasons. The activities are intended to target victims who are affected negatively by the conflict consequences and they are expecting you to provide them with physical protection. The existence of social traditions can be problematic; for example, traditions prohibit discussion of issues related to sexual violence, and thus you have difficulties to communicate with the victims. The last and important challenge is the high level of illiteracy among local groups.

In response, you need to exert creative efforts in order to overcome such difficulties by adopting innovative methods such as working to:

- Cooperate with the local administration and build trust with them in order to get access to victims;
- Work cooperatively with international organisations working on the ground, especially those who provide relief services;
- Enhance victims' participation, which requires efforts to show the positive impact of their participation;
- Adopt a simplified training approach based on role play and showing films to overcome the illiteracy issue;
- Provide pick up for participants from their locations to the training venue and provide a secure venue for training;
- Provide a place for breastfeeding mothers to feed their infants.

TCPs are not replacing activities of human rights monitoring and reporting but rather they complement these. From an individual experience, technical cooperation programmes have contributed in building the capacities of duty bearers to know their responsibilities and obligations at the same time it has contributed in raising victims' awareness in understanding their rights and thus their ability to defend them.

Training of journalists on a Human Rights-Based Approach (HRBA) for media coverage: Middle East and North Africa

In working to mobilise important groups to protect and promote human rights, I would like to reflect on my works and engagement with journalists and prominent media institutions in the Middle East and North Africa (MENA) region to promote and protect human rights. A training programme has been developed in partnership with different media institutions[2] and in cooperation with the UN Training and Documentation Centre for South West Asia and the Arab Region. The programme aimed at building the capacities of journalists on how to report human rights stories from a perspective of human rights.

From 2010 to 2015 the partners have organised a yearly programme for journalists for the MENA region. They were trained on the content of international human rights law, basic human rights conventions and additional optional protocols, obligations of the state to respect human rights, and how journalists can benefit from the protection provided by international human rights law. They were also sensitised to relevant alarming human rights issues in the MENA region, like the status of freedom of expression and it's relation to the work of a journalist, the right to access information, and the concept of transitional justice, as many countries in the region are going through transitional justice processes to deal with past human rights violations and crimes.

Journalists have also been provided a technical training on the content of HRBA, as in each story they have to reflect relevant international human rights conventions, and the concepts of non-discrimination, participation, and promotion of the rule of law. In the beginning, targeting journalists was a difficult and challenging task. Many academic and educational institutions do not provide human rights teaching for journalists during their university or training phases. The majority of teaching and training received has focused on building skills for journalistic coverage without linking this to human rights. Even a journalist who is not oriented as a human rights defender has a moral responsibility to promote and protect human rights.

The recent approach which has been adopted by many media institutions such as the Al Jazeera channel has a tangible contribution in promoting the role of journalists in human rights protection. In addition, the presence and belief

---

2   These include the Doha Centre for Media Freedom (http://www.dc4mf.org/ar) and Public Freedoms and Human Rights at Al Jazeera (http://www.aljazeera.net/news/humanrights).

of persons[3] who have a human rights background in addition to their work within these institutions has also provided additional opportunities to support the involvement of journalists in human rights issues.

The organisation of continuous yearly training programmes has resulted in creating individuals and groups of professional journalists in different media outlets in the region who are active contributors in promoting human rights. They are active journalists in newspapers like El Ghad, Al Quds, Annahar, ALQabas, Al Jazeera channel and other news agencies in Yemen, Sudan, Egypt and Algeria.[4]

Today, those trained journalists are forming themselves into networks and groups using social media to communicate and share information between them. They have also produced very strong media reports and stories, covering many important human rights issues such as child protection, combating trafficking, the status and condition of prisons, rights of women in education, the right to health and the right to education. In doing so, journalists have reflected clearly the language of human rights by using precise terms and making references to many human rights conventions and UN bodies.

Building national capacities in the field of human rights: Kingdom of Saudi Arabia

A TCP entitled 'Enhance national capacities to promote and protect human rights'[5] has been signed and agreed between the UN Office of the High Commissioner for Human Rights and the Kingdom of Saudi Arabia through the Saudi Human Rights Commission (SHRC).[6]

In its first year, the programme has carried out a series of promotional human rights activities that targeted both governmental bodies and civil society actors. A five day programme focused on the international system of human rights and its protection mechanisms has been carried out and aimed at enhancing better engagement between Saudi Arabia and the UN human rights system. The launch of the training programme was well received and got proper media coverage. It was an encouraging step to go ahead with other planned

---

3   A prominent role has been played by Dr. Hassan Mujamer, who is a Producer for the Al Jazeera channel, to support the engagement of journalists in human rights programmes and activities.

4   See the *El Ghad* newspaper in Jordan http://www.alghad.com; *AlQuds* newspaper http://www.alquds.com; *Annahar* http://www.annahar.com; *AlQabas* http://www.alqabas.com.kw.

5   A memorandum of Understanding has been signed between OHCHR and Saudi Arabia in 2012. The purpose is to build national capacities through a three-year work plan.

6   *The Saudi Human Rights Commission* is not accredited by the International Accreditation Committee – ICC.

activities. In Saudi Arabia and other countries, the availability of political will is a crucial step to plan and implement activities related to the promotion and protection of human rights.

Other subsequent activities focused on very important issues related to combating human trafficking, and the reporting mechanism for the UN Committee on the Elimination of Racial Discrimination and the UN Committee on the Elimination of Discrimination against Women. The first year of the project was concluded by organising a training-of-trainers programme which resulted in having 20 trainers, constituted by ten female and ten male participants.

The first year of implemented activities has paved the way for more constructive activities. Two training activities have targeted separately researchers working in the offices of the SHRC and another workshop for civil society activists on how to monitor and report human rights issues in Saudi Arabia. At the time of writing these lines, the project is in the last stages to organise a three day training workshop on the drafting process of the State periodic report for the Committee on the Elimination of Racial Discrimination.

Conclusion

Technical Cooperation Programmes have an important role in promoting and protecting human rights. They could be implemented during the time of conflict or in a stable situation. Countries also play an important role in fully cooperating with TCPs and not imposing restrictions to hinder its goals and objectives. To make TCPs successful, the concerns and needs of victims should be considered. This requires a measure to build trust with victims or those affected by the conflict. TCPs also should take into consideration social circumstances especially when tackling issues and programmes to combat sexual violence against women because in some societies discussing such issues is a taboo.

TCPs normally face various difficulties in both stable and non-stable countries, especially when there is doubt on the idea of human rights, or the idea of human rights clashes with culture, religion and other traditions. However, numerous experiences of TCPs should be discussed, studied and further researched as part of the requirements of academic programmes. This will identify reasons of success and failure especially in countries which are in transition or in conflict, because where there is a conflict, there will be victims of human rights.

As an individual and in order to achieve success in carrying out tasks and responsibilities within TCPs, there is a need to be equipped with a solid knowledge of human rights, and have multiple protection skills and a good understanding of the international system for human rights protection. In this regard, the MA in Understanding and Securing Human Rights has provided me with three main elements: 1) the idea of human rights and its historical philosophy and development; 2) techniques and skills for protection; and 3) familiarity with the UN human rights system.

12

Poetry for human rights

Laila Sumpton

This is perhaps not the chapter you were expecting to find in this book, for how can an art have a practical application in the territory of human rights education, campaigning and programming? I would argue that any art can be applied with a human rights-based approach, but that the compact, urgent and linguistically layered nature of poetry suits human rights work well.

I will look at 'Poetry for human rights' from three perspectives: poetry for personal resilience; poetry for human rights education and campaigning; and poetry for voice and empowerment, which charts my own journey into this area of work.

Poetry for personal resilience

Many people turn to poetry in times of crisis. Either they will read another's work or write their own – trying to condense what is happening to them, make sense of it and bear witness through writing. Being able to write about an experience acknowledges its reality, even when done through metaphor and the mirroring of characters. There is always something of ourselves in our writing, even when we tell someone else's story. On a personal level, being able to turn to writing has enabled me to process life events that would have otherwise disrupted my work and study.

On a professional and academic level, being able to turn to poetry has helped me understand key themes within human rights from genocide, to indigenous rights and refugee law, as it forces you to find the essence of injustice and explain it in words that can be understood outside the lecture hall. This has empowered me as a campaigner, even if the poems I wrote were initially just for myself. Being able to do this was particularly important when working in Bosnia with arts and human rights NGO Most Mira, firstly as an intern, then as a trustee. For the first time in my life I was directly hearing the stories of survivors of concentration camps, visiting mass graves, while at the same time organising youth arts projects and negotiating with local stakeholders.

Compartmentalising my reactions to the very present history not only enabled me to deliver projects, but also to find a way to take these stories to poetry audiences in the UK who knew little about the conflict. The poems were my awareness raising tools and the very act of writing freed the stories from my mind, allowing me to switch between Bosnia, my job at the time writing up stories about abuse suffered by young homeless people for Depaul UK, and the world of my friends and family.

Building your own resilience in the field of human rights work is crucial; everyone will have their own means. Once I had taught myself how to process information and transform it into poetry I felt better able to try and teach others how to do the same in a way that respects the dignity and agency of those you seek to represent. This led me to think about what a human rights-based approach to creative campaigning could be, and the responsibility that writers have to handle their subject matter with care and respect. I feel that artists have a responsibility to use their platforms to report the injustices they see, and to do what they can to help others raise their voice, whether they are the survivors or those who are simply aware and looking for a way to speak out.

Poetry for campaigning and human rights education

Whilst studying at the Institute of Commonwealth Studies, I was lucky to work alongside committed and engaged students who constantly debated human rights issues both in and out of the classroom. Wanting to share this outside of Senate House was something I was passionate about doing, so I set myself a challenge: turning a friend's dissertation about the refugee crisis on the Italian island of Lampedusa into a 30-line poem. How to go about this? The poem needed an approach that did not turn to sentimentality, use dry legal language or shock tactics, but would reach the people who usually switch channel when a news story becomes too distressing. My response lay in mirroring – depicting migration and the search for safety and survival as a natural process through the image of a turtle dragging herself onto a beech to lay her eggs, titled 'Landing on Lampedusa' (Sumpton 2014).

Since writing this poem in 2012, I have led a series of poetry workshops on approaches to creative campaigning with museums, youth groups, universities and a Quaker group looking at women's rights, free speech, and refugee rights through metaphor, hyperbole, satire and through manipulating legal language to make 'found poems.' Supporting learners to create well-crafted poetry that vividly describe human rights stories without resorting to propaganda and soap-box tactics is a campaign tool that helps writers to find their more political voices and to learn how to keep their audiences on side. NGOs and human rights activists can do more to share their stories with artists who can transport these issues to new ears.

Being a co-editor of the Human Rights Consortium's first poetry anthology *In Protest: 150 Poems for Human Rights* (Abelvik-Lawson, Hett and Sumpton 2013) taught me so much about the many ways in which human rights issues can be successfully voiced through poetry. We asked for submissions of human rights poetry, not knowing what we would receive, and found ourselves reading 640 entries from 14 different countries tackling a diverse range of issues ranging from land rights in rural India, to child rights in Papua New Guinea, to stories of life under Franco's rule. We set up our own grading scales for successful poems that were well crafted, clearly investigated a human rights issue and brought a fresh perspective to the debates. Over the past few years, it has been great to see how the poetry community can mobilise quickly to fund and create new anthologies whether it is responding to the imprisoning of Pussy Riot (Lucas 2012), in solidarity with the current refugee crisis (Poems For People 2015) or for the general election (Piercey and Wright 2015).

Poets can work as reporters – capturing protests, taking testimony – but they can also work as historians by linking up the stories of the past with themes in our present. In 2012, I and a fellow member of Keats House Poets worked with the Senate House archives to create new poetry for the School of Advanced Study's contribution to the Bloomsbury Festival. We used archive material detailing the University of London's approach to mobilising support for Czech student refugees in the early 1950s, and accounts from the newly arrived students themselves. Forgotten stories of past support can be bought to life through vivid poems to raise awareness of the current refugee crisis and the need for higher education bodies to contribute, as they once did.

Don Patterson, my poetry lecturer at the University of St Andrews, once said that the poem is the only art form that you can carry in your mind in its entirety. It is with this in mind that poetry can be a powerful human rights education tool. Building on several years of writing poems inspired by my work with Most Mira, this summer I led a workshop at their peacebuilding residential programme for young Bosnian and international campaigners with Humanity in Action. The session helped the learners condense what they had learned about peace processes and memorialisation at the community level into short poems, and also helped them to imagine possible futures through focussing on a ruined home that the charity hopes to turn into an arts centre (Sumpton 2015a). This session gave them the space to reflect personally on all of the visits to memorials, reburials and lectures on transitional justice and capture what they needed to tell those who had not experienced this learning for themselves. Poetry helped these campaigners work together and individually to work out what peacebuilding meant to them, and how to use what they had seen to evidence their points in an engaging, lyrical and inspiring way.

Poetry for voice and empowerment

At a conference for artists working with young people at London Theatre Bubble, one contributor mentioned something which made me question the validity and ethics of what I consider to be arts projects for social change. They spoke about the danger of artists being accidental therapists in hit and run arts projects. With the reality of funding for both arts and human rights projects being scarce, a one off session, or three to six week projects with vulnerable learners, is becoming common.

Poets sent into schools, prisons, care homes or hospitals to briefly inject creativity into the setting can help learners express themselves and raise their voices about the issues that concern them if this is followed up and part of a holistic program. Very often there is limited or no training on the support needs of the learners of safeguarding, and the artist is presumed to be safe, sensible and sensitive. Often we are, but I have been in workshops where the boundary between poetry facilitator and therapist is blurred. Well planned and supported projects with adequate time funded for reflection, training and planning avoid this, along with a good selection process.

Arts projects can empower learners, helping them express themselves, build confidence and sometimes raise their voices as campaigners. Writers' development agency Spread the Word specialises in taking literature to those who would not normally be able to access it. The right to participation and the right to a cultural life springs to mind as key areas this arts work supports. I have run poetry workshops with dialysis patients at St George's Hospital and in the paediatric wards of the Royal London Hospital and seen first-hand how moods, communication skills, willingness to work with education and health staff and confidence can improve from a few sessions (Sumpton 2015b).

The concentrated, resource light and narrative aspect of poetry sees it as a great tool for helping marginalised members of our society raise their voices and feel like they have some agency over how their stories and perspectives are told. This year I worked with Sense, the UK charity that supports people who are deaf, blind and have multiple and complex disabilities. I was tasked with delivering six months of creative writing workshops with learners in Greenwich and Spalding on the theme of local heritage and rivers, preparing them for a public performance. With the support of excellent freelance project manager Poppy Szaybo and some incredible support staff, I learned the basics of sign language and learned as I went how to creatively engage learners who had never created poetry or stories (Sense 2015). I quickly learned that I would need to write songs, as writing was not an option for the majority of learners. Yet even with all of these new ways of working I was amazed at the changes in confidence, mood management and memory amongst learners. They had never been challenged creatively in this way before or asked to imagine characters, and students who had never spoken to their peers began communicating. Again, what may have seemed like a 'decorative' arts project to some, was actually transformative and empowering for the learners. The best advocates are the clients themselves, and if arts workshops can help them grow in confidence and eventually be able to tell their story in a way that suits them, then more campaigns teams should be advocating for these kinds of projects.

From the various projects I have been a part of I have seen how poetry and story writing workshops can help learners understand and feel a sense of ownership over their own stories, and sense the validity of their own voice when they feel disempowered. Poetry can support human rights projects in many different contexts- strengthening voices of protest, voices of witnesses and voices of human rights defenders. Going forward I would ask how can we protect the right to a cultural life for marginalised people and help artists and human rights workers better collaborate? Our work runs off stories and we all need to be powerful storytellers.

Here is the poem I wrote to summarise the experience of the 2015 Project on Peacebuilding residential programme and the stories of survival we heard from Most Mira founder and Omarska camp survivor, Kemal Pervanic.

Julys near Omarska

Sleep was hard to find
for the two hundred men
locked in a steel mine room-
only space to crouch and lean
till bodies thinned, faces dwindled.

In our July, over 20 years on,
a few miles from that mine
and the tracks that had towed
the village apart
it was hotter than any July
and sleep was hard to find.

Our well ran dry, sheets dank,
and flies swarmed in heavy nights
riddled with rooster caws
and wartime tales that we
had woken, that should not sleep-
should walk pages and paths
spiralling out of here.

We had flown in from our various towns
found ourselves at a forgotten stop
on the most deadly Bosnian road
where cars swerve and flowers frame dry ditches.
We left all our shoes at the door
to contemplate their trails and shelter bugs,

as we moved onto the same carpet
we would unravel together.

We were waking up stories people pass-
whilst hay is turned, cats creep up on meat,
and the village rebuilds each year,
it's families returning to repaint doors,
teach children how to tractor lawns,
learn their accent back,
wander new old streets.

We paused and circled graves,
the roll call banners
in steel, marble, cement
with a scattering of wreaths,
stone address cards with only struck out names
re-etched and welded on a roller-deck of loss.

We look for traces, of what was there before
turned over leaves,
found jokes under forgotten bricks,
laughter where washing was hung-
birds soaring through invisible walls,
and rebuilt it all in our various tongues
to fly and carry home.

Bibliography

Abelvik-Lawson, H., A. Hett and L. Sumpton (eds.) (2013) *In Protest: 150 Poems for Human Rights* (London: Human Rights Consortium, School of Advanced Study).

Lucas, C. (2012) 'Catechism: poems for Pussy Riot Live', in *English PEN,* available at http://www.englishpen.org/events/catechism-poems-for-pussy-riot-live/ (accessed 5 Oct. 2015).

Piercey, R. and E. Wright (eds.) (2015) *Campaign in Poetry* (London: The Emma Press).

Poems For People (2015) 'Poems 4 People Anthology: in solidarity w/ refugees', in *Crowd Funder,* available at http://www.crowdfunder.co.uk/poems-4–people-anthology-in-solidarity-wrefugees (accessed 5 Oct. 2015).

Sumpton, L. (2014) 'Laila Sumpton – Landing on Lampedusa', in *IndieFeed-Performance Poetry,* available at http://indiefeedpp.libsyn.com/laila-sumpton-landing-on-lampedusa (accessed 5 Oct. 2015).

— (2015a) 'Day 3: Art and Activism', in *Humanity in Action Project on Peacebuilding,* available at https://hiapeacebuilding.wordpress.com/2015/07/23/day-3–art-activism/ (accessed 5 Oct. 2015).

— (2015b) 'Three tips for writers working with hospitals', in *Spread the Word*, available at http://www.spreadtheword.org.uk/resources/view/three-tips-for-writers-working-with-hospitals (accessed 30 Sept. 2015).

Sense (2015) *'Poems of the River' an inspiring exhibition at Ayscoughfee Hall Museum*, available at https://www.sense.org.uk/content/poems-river-inspiring-exhibition-ayscoughfee-hall-museum (accessed 5 Oct. 2015).

13

Transnational business human rights regulations and their effects upon human rights protection

Sumi Dhanarajan

Contemporary corporate-related human rights abuses are often attributed to the processes of neo-liberal globalisation.[1] Pressures upon nations to compete in the global marketplace, upon suppliers to produce ever-cheaper and ever-faster, upon workers to accept more precarious terms of employment and upon communities to give up land and natural resources, all in the pursuit of economic growth have unveiled examples of the darker side of business operations within the global economy. Whereas this side was more hidden and less susceptible to resistance in a different era, transnational activism in this age – with the aid of new forms of communication technology and media – has enabled greater public awareness of this miscreant behaviour and the ensuing injustices.

Consequently, demands have been placed upon governance systems to provide the necessary controls and protections to allay the growing problem of human rights abuses occurring as a result of business activities. Transnational business human rights regulatory regimes ('TBHRs') have emerged as a means of managing the human rights impact of global corporate activity. This form of regulatory governance is often described as a necessary 'gap-filler' (Ruggie 2013). Promoted as an interim solution to the problem of unfettered adverse business human rights impact in the apparent absence of adequate state-based measures, it is assumed that TBHRs fill a regulatory void.

---

1 I define neo-liberal globalisation as globalisation deriving from the 'Washington Consensus' that promotes trade and financial liberalisation, privatisation and deregulation, openness to foreign direct investment, a competitive exchange rate, fiscal discipline, lower taxes and small government. Transnational business governance is associated with this agenda by enabling it through self-regulation and minimal state intervention (Tabb 2005). The typologies of globalisation and the definition of neo-liberal globalisation in the context of human rights are discussed extensively in O'Connell (2007).

This assumption is somewhat misleading. In fact, TBHRs emerge into a space already occupied by state-based law and institutions, albeit that these may be currently weak or inefficient, or simply untested. Understood in this way, the emergence of TBHRs raises questions about the effects and implications of the interactions these regulatory instruments have with extant rights-protecting laws. Yet the nature and outcomes of the interactions between TBHRs and law remain understudied even though they may prove to be a critical indicator of how human rights discourse evolves in 'globalised' States in which non-state actors play a prominent role in formulating norms and implementing regulation relating to human rights.

The emergence of transnational business human rights regulation

TBHRs – a form of transnational business governance or transnational private regulation – have emerged as a means of managing the unfettered adverse human rights impact of global corporate activity, as well as a way to secure businesses' social license to operate in the globalised context. Their application reflects a broader trend towards normalising private rule-making across various regulatory spheres. In the absence of an 'overarching global political regime' (Haufler 2000) to manage complex issues such as business-related human rights abuses, the shift away from state-based rule-making is seen as inevitable (Barendrecht 2013). The 'regulatory fracture' of the global economy wherein industries involved in highly globalised systems of production are beyond the state's current regulatory reach contribute to this perception (de Sousa Santos and Rodriguez-Garavito 2005).

The emergence of TBHRs thus reflects three drivers. First, a perception that states either lack the institutional capabilities and capacities to address the problem satisfactorily or, are committed to neo-liberal deregulatory policies that demand non-state regulatory instruments (Bartley 2003). Second, the corporate imperative to respond efficiently with risk management tools that can either quell the ensuing reputational damage or ensure the viability of business operations in the face of social resistance, or to deflect state-based regulation. Third, pressure from transnational advocacy movements to seek out means of holding corporations to account for human rights violations relating to their operations.

We can observe these drivers playing out in many developing, globalising States where human rights abuses resulting from business activity are prevalent. Key industries harbour systemic human rights challenges, for example, poor working conditions in low-cost manufacturing, or disputes over natural resources and land resulting in violence, displacements and violations of civil, cultural, economic, political and social rights. Existing legal provisions either fail to comprehensively cover the facts of the claim or are weakly enforced. In these situations, the business-operating environment can permit companies to be less responsive to human rights issues. Further, victims of human rights face significant barriers to accessing legal remedies to either prevent further harm or to gain compensation or reparation for harm caused.

In the face of these challenges, transnational advocacy groups have supported local civil society in raising awareness at the domestic and global level, calling for increased corporate accountability. Under this spotlight, multinational corporations as well as larger domestic companies implicated in these rights abuses have, in some instances, sought out TBHRs as either a superficial means of cover, or in a genuine effort to understand and address the problems before they begin to pose material risks to the business. Likewise, communities, in tandem with civil society organisations, have also sometimes looked to TBHRs as a more accessible means of seeking remedy.

TBHRs take various forms: self-regulating instruments such as corporate codes of conduct that are designed and implemented by companies themselves to ensure their own as well as their supply-chain partners' compliance with human rights standards; regulatory regimes implemented through multi-stakeholder initiatives involving companies and other actors such as non-governmental organisations (examples include the Roundtable on Sustainable Palm Oil, the Ethical Trading Initiative or the Voluntary Principles on Security and Human Rights); or compliance mechanisms implemented by international or regional financial institutions which build in social and environmental impact assessment requirements into approval processes for loans and partnerships, such as the Compliance Advisory Ombudsman for the International Finance Corporation. Ever-new species of TBHRs proliferate to address the variety of issues and dynamics in the business and human rights space.

Proponents of this trend towards transnational private regulation believe that these mechanisms bring the benefits of plurality: different types of rule-making and the increase in rule-making capacity can mean thicker protection for human rights (Barendrecht et al. 2013). Further, TBHRs are seen to be more efficient and more flexible than state-based regulation, the latter being unduly constraining in achieving rights-based solutions when the abuses in question involve complex situations (Rees 2012). An often quoted example is that of child labour, where mediation-based mechanisms may achieve better outcomes by taking into account the reasons why the child is working and finding appropriate solutions in ways that litigation may not.

Those more circumspect about TBHRs question whether these mechanisms are accountable to victims, whether the voluntary nature of some of the mechanisms prevents enforceability, and whether the imbalances of power between the victims and the companies distort the fairness of the processes (Deva 2012). Skeptics question the effects of TBHRs upon social change asking, for example, if they encourage States to further renege on their duties to protect human rights against corporate abuses (Perez 2011).

In any case, the place of TBHRs within the business and human rights landscape is quite secure. Indeed the *UN Guiding Principles on Business and Human Rights*, endorsed by the UN Human Rights Council in 2011, support the use of TBHRs as a means to deliver due diligence as well as access to remedy, both being obligations associated with the Principles' requirements of meeting the corporate responsibility to respect human rights and of ensuring greater access by victims to effective grievance mechanisms.[2]

For better or worse?

The problem, however, is that analysis of TBHRs is focused mainly upon investigating whether they are in and of themselves effective regulatory instruments (that is, assessing the efficiency of these instruments in ensuring compliance or legitimacy) or whether they provide adequate access to remedies to victims. In both regards, they are often juxtaposed against state-based laws or legal institutions for rights-protection, assessed as either better than, or worse than the latter. There are, however, shortcomings in conceptualising TBHRs as part of a wider human rights ecosystem whereby their introduction, as a new species of regulatory regime, may effect the nature and functioning of other existing regimes as well as that of the ecosystem as a whole.

In effect, TBHRs pluralise human rights protection by introducing into a traditionally public terrain alternative private fora for determining applicable human rights norms and standards and for adjudicating or mediating disputes arising in connection with corporate-related rights abuses. Not examining their pluralising effects precludes an understanding of whether the systemic impact of having TBHRs is net-beneficial or net-detrimental to protection against or remedy of corporate-related human rights abuses. Ignoring the question of how TBHRs interact with other rights-related regimes makes it difficult to ascertain whether they actually enhance, complement, support, marginalise or undermine the latter, or importantly, to assess the implications of any of these possible relational effects upon rights discourse and praxis.

TBHRs, the role of law and the meaning of human rights

The role of law in protecting against and remedying corporate-related human rights abuses is in a state of flux. As suggested earlier, TBHRs are most often justified on the basis that the law has failed. The relatively slow evolution of law to address business and human rights can be, in part, traced back to normative and doctrinal barriers to finding non-state actors responsible for human rights violations. Consequently, most legal challenges have been based

2   *Guiding Principles on Business and Human Rights: Implementing the United Nations "Protect, Respect and Remedy" Framework*, U.N. Doc. A/HRC/17/31 (Mar. 21, 2011) (by Professor John Ruggie) [hereinafter 'The Guiding Principles'].

on civil, criminal law, or administrative law,[3] rather than claims for breaches of fundamental freedoms or rights protected under national constitutions or international human rights law. In pursuing such cases, whereas the harm may be 'named' as human rights abuse, the 'claiming' process in the dispute usually veers aware from addressing it as such[4] (Felstiner et al. 1980). For example, in a tort claim, the injury may be presented as trespass to the person or the claim framed as negligence. According to McCorquodale, one consequence of this phenomenon may be that 'we lose the powerful, challenging idea of human rights' when legal challenges are framed without human rights-related legislation or international conventions.[5]

Further, in making these claims numerous doctrinal and evidential obstacles present. There are also the overwhelming practical barriers to accessing the judicial system ranging from lack of financial resources, to simply lacking the capabilities to engage the legal system (Taylor et al. 2009). Having said this, there is an 'expanding web of liability' (Thompson, Ramasastry and Taylor (2009) cited by Zerk 2014, 14) for corporate abuses of human rights and there continue to be efforts to test and engage the law's muscle in addressing these contemporary human rights challenges presented by corporate-related harms. At the international level, the current process in the UN Human Rights Council to explore an international treaty represents one such effort. As the law is evolving within a regulatory space occupied – indeed prominently so – by TBHRs, it is important to think about what influence or impact these may have upon its development. As a human rights advocate, my particular interest is in how TBHRs affect the development of law as a counter-hegemonic force. *(ruling)*

There are a number of ways in which TBHRs could affect the role of law – and the meaning of human rights – through their presence and interactions with it. For example, where the law provides few reference points for their decision-making, judges may reference or even show deference to the processes and outcomes of alternative dispute resolution proceedings provided by the TBHR where these are seen as relevant to a case before them[6] and especially

---

3   For a comprehensive account of these, see Zerk (2014) and Skinner, McCorquodale, and De Schutter (2014).

4   An exception to this may be the Alien Tort Claims Act cases where the US district courts have original jurisdiction of any civil action by an alien for a tort where that tort is committed in violation of the law of nations or a treaty of the United States.

5   Presentation by Professor Robert McCorquodale, Director of the British Institute for International and Comparative Law at a Seminar on Transnational Corporate Human Rights Abuses: Delivering Access to Justice, London, UK, 17 July 2014.

6   Known as 'legal endogeneity', the concept developed by Lauren Edelman and her collaborators (Edelman et al. 2011) suggests that law acquires meaning from (and in this way becomes endogenous to) the social arenas it seeks to regulate. Her research considered how organisations that actively participate in the construction of the meaning of compliance with the law generate "ideologies of rationality" which in

where the norms and standards set by TBHRs become ubiquitous with the site or type of grievance.[7]

TBHRs may influence rights mobilisation; for example, activists may disengage with the legal regime, preferring recourse to TBHR norms and processes as a way of confronting or resolving grievances involving affronts to human dignity or, alternatively, may be encouraged to pursue litigation having had negative experiences with TBHRs. In framing a grievance, activists may choose to amalgamate norms from both TBHRs as well as the law so as to generate hybrid understandings of rights in their rights mobilisation. TBHRs may influence rights consciousness, that is the way individuals and communities think about and act towards human rights, affecting the way they understand, engage with or use the law to protect their rights (Engel 2012; McCann 2012). TBHRs may hamper the transformative or counter-hegemonic potential of the law by shifting the articulation of the scope of rights, their protection and their remedy from a public into a private space. This could 'create an illusion of accountability and thus reduce the demand for actual change' (Chesterman 2011, 63) that may arguably be better secured through litigation. Alternatively, they may actually encourage the transformative potential by offering new visions of how human rights could be reflected in law.

The point is little light is shed on the interactions between TBHRs and legal regimes. Whilst policy-makers actively promote TBHRs in line with a paradigmatic shift from government to governance, scant attention is being paid to the systemic effects and implications relating to their implementation upon the role of law and the meaning of human rights in contemporary practice. Deepening our understanding of these would be an important gauge of the future of human rights protection in our globalised world.

Bibliography

Barendrecht M., D. Raic and S. Muller (2012) *Rulejungling: When lawmaking goes private, international and informal. The HIIL Trend Report,* available at http://www.hiil.org/publication/trend-report-rulejungling (accessed 30 Sept. 2015).

Bartley, T. (2003) 'Certifying forests and factories: states, social movements and the rise of private regulation in the apparel and forest product fields', *Politics and Society* 31, pp. 433–64.

---

turn, legitimate and reinforce particular compliance strategies in the social field, something to which courts and other legal actors may well respond.

7   An example of this is perhaps the norm of free, prior and informed consent that has been developed predominantly within TBHRs, and may have some influence over how judges interpret the constitutional rights elements in land disputes over mining or agricultural concessions.

Chesterman, S. (2011) 'Laws, standards and voluntary guidelines', in G. Nystuen, A. Follesdal and O. Mestad (eds.), *Human Rights, Corporate Complicity and Disinvestment* (Cambridge: Cambridge University Press).

de Sousa Santos, B. and C. A. Rodriguez-Garavito (2005) 'Law, politics and the subaltern in counter-hegemonic globalisation', in B. de Sousa Santos and C. A. Rodriguez-Garavito (eds.), *Law and Globalisation From Below: Towards a Cosmopolitan Legality* (Cambridge: Cambridge University Press).

Deva, S. (2012) *Regulating Corporate Human Rights Violations* (Abingdon: Routledge).

Eberlein, B., K. W. Abbott, J. Black, E. Meidinger and S. Wood (2013) *Transnational Business Governance Interactions: Conceptualisation and Framework for Analysis,* available at http://digitalcommons.osgoode.yorku.ca/scholarly_works/3 (accessed 30 Sept. 2015).

Edelman, L.B., L. H. Krieger, S. R. Eliason, C. R. Albiston and V. Mellema (2011) 'When organizations rule: judicial deference to institutionalised employment structures', *American Journal of Sociology* 117 (3), pp. 888–954.

Engel, D. M. (2012) 'Vertical and horizontal perspectives on rights consciousness', *Indiana Journal of Global Legal Studies* 19 (2), pp. 423–55.

Felstiner, W., R. Abel and A. Sarat (1980/81) 'The emergence and transformation of disputes: naming, blaming and claiming', *Law & Society Review* 15 (3/4), p. 631.

Haufler, V. (2000) 'Private sector international regimes' in R. Higgot, G. Underhill and A. Bieler (eds.), *Non-state Actors and Authority in the Global System* (London: Routledge).

Levy, D. L. and R. Kaplan (2008) 'Corporate social responsibility and theories of global governance: strategic contestation in global issue arenas', in A. Crane, A. McWilliams, D. Matten and J. Moon (eds.), *Oxford Handbook of Corporate Social Responsibility* (Oxford: Oxford University Press).

McCann, M. (1994) *Rights at Work: Pay Equity Reform and the Politics of Legal Mobilization* (Chicago, IL: University of Chicago Press).

O'Connell, P. (2007) 'On reconciling irreconcilables: neo-liberal globalisation and human rights', *Human Rights Law Review* 7 (3), pp. 483–509.

Rees, C. (2012) *Mediation in Business-related Human Rights Disputes: Objections, Opportunities and Challenges, Corporate Social Responsibility Initiative Working Paper No. 56* (JFK School of Government. Harvard University).

Ruggie, J.G. (2013) *Just Business: Multinational Corporations and Human Rights. Norton Global Ethics Series* (New York: W.W. Norton & Company).

Skinner, G., R. McCorquodale and O. De Schutter (2014) *The Third Pillar: Access to Judicial Remedies for Human Rights Violations by Transnational Business* (The International Corporate Accountability Roundtable (ICAR), CORE and The European Coalition for Corporate Justice (ECCJ)).

Tabb, W. K. (2005) *Economic Governance in the Age of Globalization* (New York: Columbia University Press.)

Taylor, M. B., R. C. Thompson and A. Ramasastry (2009) *Overcoming Obstacles to Justice: Improving Access to Judicial Remedies for Business Involvement in Grave Human Rights Abuses* (Amnesty International and FAFO).

Zerk, J. (2014) *Corporate Liability for Gross Human Rights Abuses: Towards a fairer and more effective system of domestic law remedies. A report prepared for the Office of the UN High Commissioner for Human Rights,* available at http://www.ohchr.org/Documents/Issues/Business/DomesticLawRemedies/StudyDomesticeLawRemedies.pdf (accessed 30 Sept. 2015).

Part 3

Translating Human Rights into Law

14

The impact of legal aid cuts on access to justice in the UK

Smita Shah

Lawyers would argue that this is an epochal moment for access to justice in the UK. Time will judge in due course; for now it worth simply setting a marker down to capture what has passed. The date to note is 1 April 2013: this was when the *Legal Aid, Sentencing and Punishment of Offenders Act 2012* (LASPO), an Act of Parliament of the United Kingdom, came into affect. LASPO changed the landscape of civil legal aid in England and Wales[1] not only in how and by whom legal aid was administered; LASPO profoundly altered what remained within scope for legal aid, taking private family law disputes such as divorce and child custody, immigration, housing, debt and social welfare and employment out of the provision of legal aid save for those cases where 'domestic violence is involved, life or liberty are at stake or people risk losing their home' (BBC 2013). The cuts were introduced with the aim to shave off £350 million from the £2 billion civil and criminal legal aid budget, primarily in civil legal aid with proposals for eventual cuts in criminal legal aid. For a nation in financially difficult times following the banking crisis of 2008 and subsequent recession, the retrenchment of the public services was bitter surgery the nation would have to endure. Why would the provision of legal aid be immune from excision?

At the time, LASPO faced an avalanche of criticism from: the judiciary; both arms of the legal profession (solicitors represented through The Law Society and barristers represented through the Bar Council); Citizens Advice Bureaux; Law Centres; the advice sector; non-governmental organisations; and eventually even the UN Committee on the Elimination of Discrimination against Women[2] for the impact such cuts would have on access to justice for the most vulnerable members of society. A deferential, conservative and competitively

---

1   Scotland and Northern Ireland are subject to their own provisions due to devolution and legal aid remains available in Scotland.
2   United Nations Committee on the Elimination of Discrimination against Women, *Concluding observations on the seventh periodic report of the United Kingdom of Great Britain and Northern Ireland*, UN Doc. CEDAW/C/GBR/CO/7 (30 July 2013).

divided profession (solicitors and barristers) unified and revolted: the Criminal Bar Association aligned itself with criminal law solicitors, while the Justice Alliance unified the civil wing of the professions and called for protests and boycotts of court proceedings, despite the threat of possible disciplinary action by the Bar Standards Board on barristers taking part.[3] The government of the day countered with accusations of self-interest and self-enrichment on the part of the legal profession.

Self-interest notwithstanding, it is worth taking a step back to consider what the United Nations *Basic Principles on the Role of Lawyers* (1990), sets out in its preamble: 'Whereas adequate protection of the human rights and fundamental freedoms to which all persons are entitled, be they economic, social and cultural, or civil and political, requires that all persons have effective access to legal services provided by an independent legal profession'. The Basic Principles set out not only the role of lawyers, their duties and responsibilities. Governmental obligations are to ensure that access is equal and effective to all persons within their territory and subject to their jurisdiction (Principle 2) and that there is sufficient funding to ensure access for those who are disadvantaged (Principle 3). Note also a special emphasis upon 'the important role of lawyers in protecting their fundamental freedoms' (Principle 4). Lawyers are the medium and the conduits to ensure access to justice.

How do LASPO legal aid reforms sit within the commitment the UK has to ensure access to justice? International human rights law has much comfort to offer here. Access to justice has commonly been thought of as a facilitative right, a right without which others cannot be enforced (Articles 2(3), 3, 26 ICCPR, Articles 5, 6 ICERD, Article 2(2) ICESCR, Article 2 CEDAW and soft law in the form of the *UN Principles and Guidelines on Access to Legal Aid in Criminal Justice System* (2012)). When placed within the menu of the rule of law principles, it has increasingly come to have a value in and of itself.

The Inter-American Court of Human Rights, in considering the American Convention on Human Rights, has pronounced that the State's failure to provide legal aid necessary to enable the effective exercise of a form of legal

---

3   BBC (2015), *Lawyers protesting outside courts over legal aid cuts* (6 Jan. 2015), available at http://www.bbc.co.uk/news/uk-25597617(accessed 8 Oct. 2015); Owen Bowcott, Peter Walker and Lisa O'Carroll (2014), 'Courts close across England and Wales as lawyers protest at legal aid cuts', *The Guardian* (6 Jan. 2014), available at http://www.theguardian.com/law/2014/jan/06/courts-close-england-wales-lawyers-legal-aid-cuts (accessed 8 Oct. 2015); James Cusick (2015), Legal aid cuts: Criminal courts across England and Wales could grind to a halt as lawyers protest, *The Independent* (26 June 2015), available at http://www.independent. co.uk/news/uk/home-news/criminal-courts-across-england-and-wales-could-grind-to-a-halt-as-lawyers-protest-legal-aid-cuts-10346409.html (accessed 8 Oct. 2015); Justice Alliance (2015), *Legal aid cuts threaten our very democracy*, available at https://justiceallianceuk.wordpress.com (accessed 8 Oct. 2015).

recourse renders that recourse illusory and that this constitutes a violation by the state of Article 1(1), 8 and 25 of the Convention (*Hilaire, Constantine and Benjamin et al v. Trinidad and Tobago* Judgement 21 June 2002).

Article 14 (3) (d) ICCPR and Article 6(3)(c) of the *European Convention for the Protection of Human Rights and Fundamental Freedoms* explicitly set out governmental obligations for the provision of legal aid in criminal justice. Jurisprudence from the European Court of Human Rights when considering Article 6(3)(c) has elaborated that this has a means (indigence) and merits (the interests of justice) test for the provision of legal aid (*Artico v. Italy*, Judgment of May 13, 1980, *Pakelli v. Germany*, Judgment of April 25, 1983 and *Quaranta v. Switzerland*, Judgment of May 24, 1991).

What of civil legal aid? In the *Airey v. Ireland*, Judgment of October 9, 1979, the European Court of Human Rights found that Article 6 (1) also implies the right to free legal assistance in certain civil cases. Mrs Airey sought free legal assistance to institute divorce proceedings against her abusive husband, who refused to sign a voluntary separation agreement. While not an absolute right, and subject to curtailment in circumstances, the Court ruled that the right applies in civil cases when such assistance proves indispensable for effective access to the courts, either because legal representation is mandatory under domestic law or because of the complexity of the procedure or the type of case. The fact is that the case concerned a marital dispute entailing emotional involvement incompatible with the level of objectivity required by advocacy in court.

Have these legal aid reforms created institutional, structural and actual barriers impeding access to justice? Sadly, many of the dire predictions came to pass: an impact assessment by Warwick University in April 2013 entitled *The State of the Sector* warned of advice deserts in patches across England and Wales (Byrom 2013). In March 2015, the Parliamentary Justice Committee reported on the impact of the changes to civil legal aid under LASPO. The Justice Committee was told that nine law centres had shut down (one in six of the law centre network members) and ten such centres run by Shelter (a homelessness charity).[4] Local Authorities have faced cuts in grants from central government and they have in turn stopped funding law centres. A Rights of Women survey found that 31.3 per cent of respondents reported that finding a legal aid solicitor in her area was difficult, with some respondents reported to having to travel between five and 15 miles to find a legal aid solicitor. Factors such as closure of legal aid law firms, legal aid departments within firms, smaller law firms merging or being swallowed by medium to larger law firms all meant

---

4   House of Commons Justice Committee, *Eighth Report of Session 2014–15, 4 March 2015: Impact of Changes to civil legal aid under Part 1 of the Legal Aid, Sentencing and Punishment of Offenders Act 2012*, available at http://www.publications.parliament. uk/pa/cm201415/cmselect/cmjust/311/31102.htm (accessed 8 Mar. 2015).

specialist solicitors who carried out legal aid work in areas such as housing, family and immigration were not longer available or accessible.

LASPO created a gateway for victims of domestic violence to be able to access legal aid, as long as they could navigate the gateway and provide evidence to demonstrate their victim status. Evidence accepted by the Justice Select Committee suggested that as many as 39 per cent of women eligible for legal aid through the domestic violence gateway were unable to access legal aid and hence justice. A Rights of Women survey carried out in 2014 reported 62.1 per cent of respondents were not already in possession of the evidence they required, and 77.8 per cent of those respondents reported that they did not know who to ask to obtain a copy of it. 22.7 per cent of respondents had to wait for longer than two weeks to receive a copy of the required evidence.[5] Women, even those on benefits, were required to pay £50 for a letter from the doctor as proof or £60 for a memorandum of conviction. Owing to the strict evidence criteria, some of those excluded are victims who reached out to women's support groups, but not to the authorities; women who called the police but whose calls were unanswered; or women who did not call the police or see a doctor, because they suffered no serious physical injuries (UNHRC 2015).

The cuts came against a backdrop marketisation of all areas of the justice system, which had been happening by stealth for a number of years (Genn 2012). Between 2006 and 2009, the legal profession and legal advice sector faced a cap in the fees regime. In 2011, there was a 10 per cent cut across the board in all areas of legal aid. The Legal Services Act 2007 enabled general legal advice to be given by non-lawyers thereby challenging the monopoly the legal profession had upon the provision of legal services. The Bar Standards Board (BSB) had started to publish a biennial survey of its profession and the background of those practising – a taking-stock exercise about the Bar and Barristers. In 2011 and 2013, the BSB found that 37 and 35 per cent of the profession were female. In 2013 and in 2011, 61 per cent of family practitioners were female, the area hardest hit by the legal aid cuts. The BSB Biennial Survey indicated that the majority of the white, male and Oxbridge-educated barristers are in chancery, commercial and privately paying areas of law, which have been traditionally difficult for women and BME (Black and minority ethnic) candidates to break into. Family, immigration, housing, and crime had been traditionally more accessible to candidates from state schools,

---

5   Right of Women's evidence to the Justice Select Committee on the impact of changes to civil legal aid under the Legal Aid, Sentencing and Punishment of Offenders Act 2012 dated April 2014, available at http://rightsofwomen.org.uk/wp-content/uploads/2014/10/Evidence-to-the-Justice-Select-Committee-on-the-impact-of-changes-to.pdf (accessed 8 Oct. 2015).

the Russell group or newer universities and are predominantly legal-aid practitioners.[6]

LASPO embraced a programme of continued privatisation of prisons (Poyner 2012), privatisation of the probation service (Travis 2014), cuts to the budget of Her Majesty's Courts and Tribunals Service (Hyde 2012; 2015), an increase in court fees for employment dispute cases, divorce applications and the on-going closure of court houses themselves (157 court houses in 2010 and a further 91 court houses proposed in July 2015) (Family Law Week n.d.; BBC 2015).

The cuts in legal aid were designed to divert people away from contentious litigation and towards mediation and alternate dispute resolution; this did not happen for the simple reason that there was no accompanying mass public awareness and education campaign. The public became aware that civil legal aid was no more and stopped going to see lawyers; they did not, to the horror of the courts, stop seeking resolution of disputes through the court. Hence the rise in litigants in person and increasing delays in court. Alternate legal services providers have sprung up to fill the void, including self-help guides available on the internet, over the telephone, or in books; unregulated services such as McKenzie Friends (who are allowed to assist but not act as lawyers in court), student law clinics and pro bono services by larger commercial law firms. The latter remains controversial within the legal profession, the dilemma being to legitimise the erosion of access to justice by filling the void left by professional flight of experienced legal aid lawyers.

How does marketisation of the justice system sit within a state obligation to ensure access to justice and legal aid? The desire on the part of successive governments has been to promote informal resolution of legal disputes, diversion away from the formal justice system and privatisation of institutions and actors. In order to achieve this, the public are required to engage with these different means of resolving legal dispute; the cuts in civil legal aid did not have the corresponding change in public behaviour. Perceptions of justice, fairness and adjudication still involve lawyers, courts and trials. The difference is now qualitative; access to justice has migrated from being an entitlement the state is obliged to provide for to an act of charity, fulfilled at the behest of the goodwill of unaccountable others. This is a precarious position for any human right to be in.

---

6 Bar Standards Board (2014), *Barristers' Working Lives: a second biennial survey of the bar 2013*, available at https://www.barstandardsboard.org.uk/media/1597662/ biennial_survey_report_2013.pdf (accessed 16 June 2015). Bar Standards Board (2012), *Barristers' Working Lives: a second biennial survey of the bar 2011*, available at https://www.barstandardsboard.org.uk/media/1385164/barristers__working_ lives_30.01.12_web.pdf (accessed 16 June 2015).

Bibliography

BBC (2013) *Q&A: Legal aid changes* (20 March 2013), available at http://www.bbc.co.uk/news/uk-21668005 (accessed 8 Oct. 2015).

Byrom, N. (2013) *The State of the Sector: The impact of cuts and civil legal aid on practitioners and her clients, A Report by the Centre for Human Rights in Practice, University of Warwick in association with illegal,* available at http://www2.warwick.ac.uk/fac/soc/law/research/centres/chrp/projects/legalaidcuts/153064_statesector_report-final.pdf (accessed 8 Oct. 2015).

Family Law Week (n.d.) *Ministry of justice proposes closure of 157 courts,* available at http://www.familylawweek.co.uk/site.aspx?i=ed60918 (accessed 8 Oct. 2015); BBC (16 July 2015), *Ninety one 'surplus' courts face closure,* available at http://www.bbc.co.uk/news/uk-33549588 (accessed 8 Oct. 2015).

Genn, H. (2012) 'Why privatisation of civil justice is a rule of law issue' F. A. Mann lecture, available at http://www.laws.ucl.ac.uk/wp-content/uploads/2014/08/36th-F-A-Mann-Lecture-19.11.12–Professor-Hazel-Genn.pdf (accessed 8 Oct. 2015).

Hyde, J. (2015) 'HMCTS reveals plans to cut 400 court jobs', *The Law Society Gazette* (22 June 2015), available at http://www.lawgazette.co.uk/news/hmcts-reveals-plans-to-cut-400–court-jobs/5049543.article (accessed 8 Oct. 2015).

Hyde, J. (2012) 'Hundreds of court posts axed', *The Law Society Gazette* (19 Jan. 2012), available at http://www.lawgazette.co.uk/news/hundreds-of-court-posts-axed/63809.fullarticle (accessed 8 Oct. 2015).

Pyner, C. (2012) 'Prison privatisation should be a national scandal', *The Guardian* (8 Nov.2012), available at http://www.theguardian.com/commentisfree/2012/nov/08/prison-privatisation-g4s-wolds (accessed 8 Oct. 2015).

Travis, A. (2014) 'Chris Grayling to press ahead with probation service privatisation', *The Guardian* (2 Dec. 2014), available at http://www.theguardian.com/society/2014/dec/02/chris-grayling-probation-service-privatisation (accessed 8 Oct. 2015).

UN Human Rights Council (UNHRC) (2015) *Report of the Special Rapporteur on violence against women, its causes and consequences, Rashida Manjoo Mission to the United Kingdom and Northern Ireland,* UN Doc. A/HRC/29/27/Add.2 (19 May 2015).

15

Remedy Australia: because every human rights violation should be remedied

Olivia Ball

> *'Any person whose rights or freedoms as herein recognised are violated shall have an effective remedy ...'*
> *– International Covenant on Civil and Political Rights*, art. 2(3)

In the 20 years the Institute of Commonwealth Studies has been teaching the MA in human rights, 40 individual complaints of human rights violations by Australia have been upheld by the UN treaty bodies. This places Australia fifth of all participating nations for adverse findings by the UN committees (behind South Korea, Jamaica, Belarus and Uruguay).[1]

Yet, even by the most generous assessment, Australia has implemented only 15 per cent of these quasi-judicial decisions. Some gross violations identified in individual communications, far from being remedied, continue unchecked.[2]

1   UN Office of the High Commissioner for Human Rights (2014), *Statistical survey of individual complaints dealt with by the Human Rights Committee* (Geneva: United Nations), available at http://www.ohchr.org/Documents/HRBodies/CCPR/StatisticalSurvey.xls (accessed 23 Sept. 2015); UN Office of the High Commissioner for Human Rights (2014), *Statistical survey of individual complaints dealt with by CERD* (Geneva: United Nations), available at http://www.ohchr.org/Documents/HRBodies/CERD/StatisticalSurvey.xls (accessed 23 Sept. 2015); UN Office of the High Commissioner for Human Rights (2015*), Status of communications dealt with by CAT* (Geneva: United Nations), available at http://www.ohchr.org/Documents/HRBodies/CAT/StatisticalSurvey.xls (accessed 23 Sept. 2015).

2   The *travaux préparatoires* of the 2005 *Basic Principles and Guidelines on the Right to a Remedy and Reparation for Victims of Gross Violations of International Human Rights Law and Serious Violations of International Humanitarian Law* (the 'Van Boven Principles') include a non-exhaustive list of gross violations: 'genocide; slavery and slavery-like practices; summary or arbitrary executions; torture and cruel, inhuman or degrading treatment or punishment; enforced disappearance; arbitrary and prolonged detention; deportation or forcible transfer of population; and systematic discrimination, in particular based on race or gender.' (T. Van Boven, *Study*

My doctoral research, which looked at the value of UN communications to the people who initiate them, may be the first systematic empirical study of authors' experience in dealing with the UN treaty bodies and the long-term outcomes of their cases.[3] To summarise my findings:

- Exhausting domestic remedies is onerous and often costly. However, most authors of individual communications would have pursued domestic remedies even without the UN requirement to do so.
- Although the communications procedure is designed to be accessible without needing a lawyer, having a lawyer is a big help.
- Authors found the communications procedures and operation of the committees difficult to understand and to follow as their case progressed, and the committees difficult to contact.[4]
- UN communications take, on average, more than three years from start to finish. Such delays pose difficulties for authors, especially those (such as detainees and deportees) experiencing gross violations of their human rights while they await an outcome.
- Although Australia has rejected almost all the committees' final views, it has, in most instances, acted on 'interim views' from the committees. These requests, seeking urgent action where irreparable harm is imminent, have most commonly asked Australia not to deport an author while their communication is underway. For refugees, this may save lives.

---

concerning the right to restitution, compensation and rehabilitation for victims of gross violations of human rights and fundamental freedoms, UN Doc E/CN4/Sub2/1993/8 (1993), principle 1.) More than half of the individual communications upheld against Australia have concerned arbitrary detention, and some of their authors, notably authors of *F.K.A.G. et al. v. Australia* and *M.M.M. et al. v. Australia*, are still detained. See the UN Human Rights Committee (2014), *General comment No. 35, Article 9 (Liberty and security of person)*, UN Doc. CCPR/C/GC/35 (16 December 2014) on what constitutes arbitrary detention.

3   In-depth interviews were conducted with 18 complainants or 'authors' of communications in which Australia was found to be in breach of its human rights treaty obligations – all those authors who could be found and who agreed to participate. Only 33 communications had been decided against Australia at that point (1994–2013), so over half of all successful authors were interviewed for this research. They commented on the risks, time, effort, expense and other costs involved in pursuing this form of remedy, relative to the outcomes achieved. See O. Ball (2013), *All the Way to the UN: Is petitioning a UN human-rights treaty body worthwhile?*, unpublished doctoral thesis, Monash Law School (Melbourne).

4   Indeed, the treaty bodies sometimes have difficulty contacting authors. Some authors had no idea they had won a human rights complaint at the UN – some had no memory of even lodging one – until a doctoral student sought to interview them about it.

- A small number of authors suffered significant negative consequences connected with their communication, such as hate mail, death threats, debt, bankruptcy, loss of employment and declining health, as well as opportunity costs while occupied with their communication.
- However, no-one felt any pressure to withdraw their UN complaint – either from the Australian government or from third parties. The evidence suggests that it is generally safe for people to petition the UN committees without fear of reprisal within Australia.[5]
- As noted above, Australia's compliance with final views of the treaty bodies has been very poor. The great majority of authors has received no substantive remedy at all.[6] Most people have great difficulty exerting effective pressure to obtain compliance with the UN's views on their case. The reasons for this vary, including relative poverty, language barriers, incarceration, mental illness, insecure migration status and, perhaps most significantly, lack of support from the human rights movement.[7]
- A very limited number of authors report positive outcomes – often unexpected or indirect – such as respect among their peers and a positive public profile contributing to their professional standing; or a sense of achievement and self-confidence in new-found abilities developed or revealed in the process of defending their rights. However, most authors interviewed reported no positive outcomes from their communication.

5 This may help explain the relatively high number of communications brought against Australia, along with the generally free access to information about communications procedures, the availability of pro bono lawyers willing to assist authors and the dominant language of Australia being a UN language. Add to this the lack of an interim stratum of a regional court of human rights in the Asia–Pacific, and people who have exhausted all domestic remedies have nowhere to go but the UN. While the risk of reprisal within Australia is low, authors seeking asylum may be placed at greater risk in their country of origin if they are identified in final views and *refouled*. Published views have revealed not only asylum seekers' identity, but also details of their family and the basis of their refugee claim. Some authors, and apparently some of their representatives, are not aware they can request anonymity from the treaty bodies.

6 In a limited sense, the verdict of a court or tribunal as to whether a human rights violation has occurred is itself a remedy. But surely the ICCPR's promise of an effective remedy means more than this. It is helpful to distinguish mere *procedural* remedies provided by courts from the *substantive* remedies which ought to follow, in which action is taken to end the violation (cessation), repair harm done (reparations) and/or prevent further violations (non-repetition).

7 A notable exception is the Australian human rights lawyers and legal academics who have represented authors. Most, if not all, have done so pro bono but few concern themselves with pursuing implementation of treaty body views.

One might expect bitterness. The surprise finding was that most authors regard their UN communication as having been worthwhile. Despite the negative consequences far outnumbering any positive outcomes, most people thought complaining to the UN had been worth it. The value to authors of vindication by one of the world's highest human rights authorities is not to be underestimated, especially as it comes after the long journey of exhausting domestic remedies and the discouragement of having 'lost' their case at every prior tribunal.

In short, victims value procedural remedies, even in the absence of substantive remedies. Which is not to say they don't want substantive remedies, but they do face formidable challenges in securing them.

The Australian experience suggests authors are more likely to obtain a substantive remedy if they are able to secure significant media coverage of their UN case; and if they have ongoing, organised support of some kind. In Australia at least, most UN communications receive very little media coverage. Without public attention on the violation, there will be no public pressure; and without pressure exerted on duty-holders, they may be unlikely to provide a remedy.

Thus there seemed to be a gap in civil society for an organisation dedicated to publicising UN communications as they arrive, monitoring the state's response to them, and exerting political pressure, where necessary, to ensure implementation of committee views. Nick Toonen and I founded such an organisation and called it Remedy Australia.

Nick Toonen is the author of the very first individual communication filed against Australia. *Toonen v. Australia* was 'a decision of historic proportions … with wide-ranging implications for the human rights of millions of people'.[8] It was exceptional in many ways, not least because it was initiated by a human rights NGO as a form of strategic litigation, backed by a long advocacy campaign for equality and justice (see box).

Toonen remains unsurpassed as the high-water mark for successful implementation of committee views in Australia. It is no accident that it resulted in substantive remedies for Mr Toonen and all LGBTI Tasmanians. No other author has had the benefit of a dedicated and determined civil society campaign to capitalise on his UN win. In contrast, most authors of communications against Australia remain disempowered, isolated and without remedy. They disappear from view, along with their case. Human rights organisations have generally failed to support authors and to capitalise on these high-level, independent pronouncements on states' human rights performance.

8   N. Pillay (2011) 'UN Human Rights Chief highlights Australian sexuality case' video address, uploaded by the Australian High Commission for Human Rights on its YouTube channel (25 July 2011), available at http://www.youtube.com/watch?v=NT5aBa-1bXs (accessed 17 Sept. 2015).

Toonen v. Australia (HRC, 1994)

Nick Toonen was a gay Tasmanian in a state where consenting sex between adult men in private was still punishable by up to 25 years' jail. Mr Toonen alleged that this violated his right to privacy and that the only effective remedy would be repeal of the relevant provisions of the *Tasmanian Criminal Code.* The Australian Government agreed with Mr Toonen, noting that homosexuality had been decriminalised in all other Australian jurisdictions. The Tasmanian Government defended its laws, however, on public health and moral grounds.

The UN Human Rights Committee (HRC) found the laws were an arbitrary interference with Mr Toonen's right to privacy and that an effective remedy would require the repeal of those laws. It also established that the prohibition on discrimination on the basis of 'sex' found in ICCPR articles 2(1) and 26 includes sexual orientation. Australia enacted the *Human Rights (Sexual Conduct) Act 1994 (Cth)* to prohibit laws that arbitrarily interfere with the sexual conduct of adults in private. Tasmania subsequently amended its *Criminal Code.*

Meanwhile, pressure on the state to provide each successful author with an effective and enforceable remedy diminishes over time.

If the UN's individual communication procedures are to be of practical value in preventing and redressing human rights violations, many countries may benefit from systematic civil society monitoring of treaty body jurisprudence and follow-up activity to ensure implementation of committee views.

Remedy Australia maintains a comprehensive online database of successful Australian communications and advocates for implementation of the remedies recommended by the committees exactly as stated in their final views. We campaign for individual remedies only with the consent of the author and/or their lawyer. The treaty bodies usually recommend guarantees of non-repetition as well, often in the form of law or policy reform. Thus remedies are not only for the individual, but should achieve broader, systemic advances in human rights protection.

In our first year, we had a significant win with *Horvath v. Australia* (see box). Working with Ms Horvath's lawyers, we mobilised thousands of supporters in an on- and off-line campaign that secured her a public apology and *ex gratia* payment as compensation, setting a new standard for timely and good-faith responses to individual communications, a mere five months after the UN Human Rights Committee's final views. The *Police Act* has also been amended, but Ms Horvath's lawyers – a community legal centre specialising in police misconduct cases – are not satisfied it goes far enough, and thus the *Horvath*

Horvath v. Australia (HRC, 2014)

During an unlawful police raid on her home, 21-year-old Corinna Horvath was thrown to the floor and punched repeatedly in the face by a policeman until she was unconscious and her nose broken. She required surgery for her injuries. The County Court found the police guilty of trespass, assault, unlawful arrest and false imprisonment, and awarded Ms Horvath compensation, but the police force denied liability and did not discipline or prosecute any of the police officers involved. Eighteen years after the assault, the HRC found that Ms Horvath's right to an effective remedy has been violated and recommended law reform and compensation.

Nystrom v. Australia (HRC, 2011)

Stefan Nystrom was born in Sweden and entered Australia as a baby only 27 days old. Mr Nystrom began hearing voices in childhood and has suffered psychiatric symptoms throughout his life. From the age of ten, he began offending, usually under the influence of alcohol, leading ultimately to terms in prison.

At the age of 30, seven years after his last offence, during which time he had been law-abiding, steadily employed and recovering from his alcoholism, Mr Nystrom's visa was cancelled on character grounds. An appeal to the Federal Court found him to be 'an absorbed member of the Australian community with no relevant ties elsewhere'. The Immigration Minister appealed successfully to the High Court, however, and in 2009 deported Mr Nystrom to Sweden. Mr Nystrom knows no-one in Sweden and, due to a learning disability, has little capacity to learn Swedish or integrate successfully. Known locally as 'The Australian', Mr Nystrom has spent years either homeless, in homeless shelters, in prison or in psychiatric care.

The HRC found Mr Nystrom's deportation constituted arbitrary interference with his right to family and (in a landmark ruling) his 'right to enter his own country', which is Australia, despite his not being an Australian citizen. Further, his expulsion was arbitrary – occurring so long after his offending. In the view of the HRC, he should be permitted and materially assisted to return to Australia. Australia has refused to allow Mr Nystrom back into Australia, but says it has made policy reforms to guard against repetition.

case is only partially remedied and we continue to campaign for further law reform.

Conversely, in the case of *Nystrom*, Australia has acted to prevent repetition, but refuses to remedy the individual violation, which Remedy Australia regards as urgent, given the violation is ongoing and given Mr Nystrom's vulnerabilities and parlous existence (see box).

Finally, in addition to publicising committee views and advocating for individual and preventive remedies, Remedy Australia seeks to close the loop by feeding information back to the UN treaty bodies. Through direct contact with authors and their representatives and systematic monitoring, we provide the UN committees with independent, accurate and up-to-date information on any progress towards implementation of each of its views, complementing and supporting the treaty bodies' own efforts at follow-up.

We welcome the establishment of sister organisations around the world. Is there a need for a branch of Remedy where you are?

16

Extraterritorial *non-refoulement*: intersections between human rights and refugee law

David James Cantor

How does international law require States acting outside their own territories to treat refugees and other persons fleeing harm in their countries?[1] This question has assumed increasing contemporary relevance in light of heightened externalised border controls, such as attempts by States to interdict migrant boats on the high seas in the Mediterranean (see, for instance Moreno-Lax 2012). However, the issue also arises in other contemporary scenarios, such as where persons seek protection in diplomatic or consular premises, where one State militarily occupies the territory of another, and where a State sets up a system for the extraterritorial processing of asylum claims.

This short analysis addresses the *non-refoulement* aspect of this extraterritoriality problem, i.e. protection against enforced removal to a territory where the person fears harm by a State acting outside its own territory. Inspired by the human rights focus of the volume overall, the chapter draws on current research by the author in order to examine this ever-topical concern against recent advances in the field of international human rights law. It not only confirms the view that the *non-refoulement* rule in human rights law applies extraterritorially, but also concludes that the resulting procedural implications should be taken seriously both for human rights law and for refugee law.

Development of human rights doctrine on 'extraterritoriality'

The many human rights treaties adopted by the United Nations (UN) and regional organisations offer a patchwork of different legal provisions for the protection of human rights by contracting States. Rather than reprise the basic elements of this framework, as the basis for subsequent discussion, the present

1   This intriguing question was recently raised by Ralph Wilde in his seminar on 'The Extraterritorial Application of the *Non-refoulement* Obligation in International Human Rights Law', 5th International Refugee Law Seminar Series, Refugee Law Initiative, School of Advanced Study, University of London. 5 May 2015.

section instead outlines two doctrinal advances concerning extraterritoriality in human rights law: the jurisdiction of States acting extraterritorially (Wilde 2003); and the prohibition of *refoulement* to human rights violations in another territory.

Extraterritorial jurisdiction of States

International treaties governing human rights usually require that a contracting State respect and ensure these rights for persons subject to their territorial jurisdiction, i.e. who are present on its territory. However, students on the MA in Human Rights who have taken the law module in recent years will (or should!) be familiar with the idea that these same States will also sometimes be required to respect and/or ensure the human rights of individuals outside their territory. Indeed, it seems that human rights obligations arise where a State exercises certain forms of authority – or 'jurisdiction' – outside its own territory. This could be on the territory of another State or outside territory claimed by any State (e.g. on the high seas).

The famous judgment of the European Court of Human Rights in *Al-Skeini and Others v. UK* identifies some scenarios in which such 'extraterritorial' jurisdiction exists. Firstly, where a State exercises effective control *over a zone* outside its national territory, whether as a consequence of lawful or unlawful military action, then it is apparently required to guarantee the full gamut of treaty rights to persons in that zone.[2] Secondly, where State officials exercise control and authority *over an individual* – whether through diplomatic/consular acts or through the use of force – then this form of jurisdiction requires that the State guarantee the rights pertinent to the situation of that individual. 'In this sense, therefore, the Convention rights can be "divided and tailored".'[3]

This rationale is largely in line with the emerging doctrine being developed by other international courts and treaty body mechanisms. It strongly suggests that human rights obligations – or at least in relation to certain rights – will remain applicable to States in certain scenarios where certain concrete acts by their agents take place, or produce effects, extraterritorially.

Refoulement to extraterritorial human rights violations

The other main area in which international human rights law has developed doctrinally in order to address issues of extraterritoriality is in relation to the principle of '*non-refoulement*'. Deriving originally from refugee law, this principle prohibits a State from removing an alien (foreigner) from its territory where this would result in serious harm to the alien *outside that territory*. However, since the 1980s, this principle has been developed considerably by international human rights law.

2   *Al-Skeini and Others v. UK*, paras 133–7.
3   Ibid., paras 138–40.

In human rights law, the *non-refoulement* principle is derived principally from the core prohibition on torture, inhuman or degrading treatment or punishment. The idea is that if it is illegal for a State to torture a person under its own jurisdiction, then equally it must be prohibited to remove him/her to another territory where s/he would be tortured. The principle finds concrete expression, *inter alia*, in Article 3 of the 1984 UN Convention Against Torture and it has been read into most other treaties that prohibit torture etc. in more general terms.[4]

The human rights *non-refoulement* principle has a strong speculative aspect, i.e. it is engaged by the envisaged risk extraterritorially. As such, it does not establish the removing State's responsibility for acts committed by others outside its territory. Rather, where the risk of serious abuse awaits the alien at the other end, the principle typifies the act of removal – initiated on the territory of the removing State – as 'degrading' or 'inhumane'.[5] For this reason, even where the abuse overseas does not take the specific form of torture but rather interference with other rights (e.g. fair trial), the *non-refoulement* principle can prevent removal where the abuse of other rights is 'flagrant'.[6]

Non-refoulement in extraterritorial contexts

Human rights law frames extraterritorial considerations according to two distinct rationales, as shown above. In the context of *refoulement*, the removing State's responsibility is engaged by its own actions on its territory albeit in light of the potential eventual consequences extraterritorially. Where a State acts outside its territory, human rights obligations bite directly wherever jurisdiction is exercised. What, though, is the legal position where both rationales apply simultaneously, i.e. where a State acting extraterritorially is faced with a situation of potential *refoulement*?

Applicability of *non-refoulement* principle extraterritorially?

The doctrinal analysis above shows that States acting extraterritorially will sometimes be exercising jurisdiction in a manner constitutive of human rights obligations. The question here is whether those obligations encompass the *non-refoulement* principle.

---

4   Thus, the European Court of Human Rights reads the principle into Article 3 of the 1950 European Convention on Human Rights in *Soering v. UK*; the Inter-American Court of Human Rights reads it into Article 5 of the 1969 American Convention on Human Rights in its *Advisory Opinion OC-21/14 on Rights and Guarantees of Children in the Context of Migration and/or in Need of International Protection*; and the Human Rights Committee reads it into Article 7 of the 1966 International Covenant on Civil and Political Rights in *Chitat Ng v. Canada*.
5   See the European Court of Human Rights in *Soering v. UK*, para. 91.
6   See the European Court of Human Rights in *Othman (Abu Qatada) v. UK*, paras. 258–85.

In principle, in the first *Al-Skeini* scenario of a State exerting effective control over a zone of another State's territory, *non-refoulement* should remain applicable alongside other human rights guarantees. Thus, in the example of military occupation, human rights law presumably should prevent an occupying State from removing a person from occupied territory where the risk of human rights abuse at the other end exists.[7]

Less straightforward is the second *Al-Skeini* scenario of the State agent(s) exerting control and authority over an individual extraterritorially. In contrast to the first scenario, the State agent(s) is/are acting in a context where the wider apparatus of their own State is not present and in control. We are thus much less likely to be talking about situations involving the 'removal of aliens' in relation to which much of the human rights *non-refoulement* doctrine has been developed. A broader spectrum of scenarios exists in which the principle of *non-refoulement* is, in the words of the *Al-Skeini* judgment, more or less relevant to the situation of that individual.

Some of these scenarios will have clear and direct parallels with the established *non-refoulement* removal paradigm. This is the case, for instance, where a State official attempts to transfer an individual under his/her power to another country (whether by kidnap or formal procedure) where the risk of harm exists. A similar scenario may be where a State official on a boat turns back, or escorts back, a boat full of migrants encountered on the open sea to a territory where they face harm. In these scenarios, the direct relationship between the act of the State agent and exposure to envisaged harm in another territory should bring the *non-refoulement* principle into play.[8]

However, in other scenarios, it may be less easy to establish a sufficiently proximate link between the extraterritorial official act and the envisaged harm necessary to engage the *non-refoulement* principle. If so, then we may see greater jurisprudential development around the legal threshold for such proximity in the future. The challenge will be particularly acute in cases that do not involve use of force against a person by a State agent but rather revolve around diplomatic or consular acts. It will be interesting to see the extent to which such developments redraw the international law parameters of diplomatic asylum, i.e. temporary asylum granted on diplomatic premises (Noll 2005).

---

7   Even if the laws of war apply simultaneously as *lex specialis*, and thus modify certain human rights obligations, the two bodies of law largely march in line in prohibiting *refoulement*. For a more detailed analysis of the position under the laws of war, see Cantor (2014).

8   This has been confirmed by the European Court of Human Rights in cases such as, respectively, *Öcalan v. Turkey* and *Hirsi Jamaa and Others v. Italy*.

Procedural implications of the applicability of the *non-refoulement* principle?

One element that is missing from much of the discussion surrounding these themes is the question of whether, or to what extent, procedural guarantees apply in this extraterritorial context. In other words, does human rights law require that certain procedural or due process guarantees must be observed by State agents acting outside their territory when deciding whether the principle of *non-refoulement* applies to a particular situation or individual? From an administrative perspective, this processual aspect is crucial since it is not usually apparent from a quick glance whether or not any individual should benefit from the *non-refoulement* rule, but rather requires deeper investigation of their particular circumstances.

Where potential *refoulement* arises in the removal context on a State's own territory, international human rights jurisprudence has increasingly adopted the consensus that the removal decision must be taken in line with due process guarantees (Cantor 2015). The various international human rights systems provide different legal bases and rationales for this development. Nonetheless, where the risk of *refoulement* is in issue, all generally require, *inter alia*, that the alien: has access to decision-making by a 'competent' national authority; independent, individual, rigorous and prompt scrutiny of the issue; automatic suspensive effect of the removal measure; a reasoned decision; and often the opportunity to challenge it at a higher instance, usually the national courts.

There is little doubt that these guarantees would apply in the first *Al-Skeini* scenario, where the State effectively continues to act as a State albeit on another State's territory. However, the implications are likely to be much more far-reaching in the second *Al-Skeini* scenario where the agent(s) of the State acting outside its territory exercise control and authority over an individual. Indeed, they would need either to be, or to have recourse to, authorities competent to evaluate these cases and take such decisions. Moreover, the requirement to do so in accordance with due process standards entails in itself access to a considerable bureaucratic (and also likely judicial) infrastructure.

For instance, where boats of migrants are intercepted and pushed back on the high seas, do these human rights guarantees require a proper decision-making process for any passengers who express or reasonably may be believed to have a fear of harm? In other words, does the full gamut of procedural guarantees applicable to *refoulement* in the context of removal apply? Recent case-law from the European Court of Human Rights suggests this question is to be answered in the affirmative, holding that the migrants' right to an effective remedy was breached by the fact that they had 'no access to a procedure to identify them and to assess their personal circumstances' before they were directed back to a territory where they faced possible harm.[9]

9   See *Hirsi Jamaa and Others v. Italy*, esp. paras. 196–207.

If correct, then in scenarios where the extraterritorial act of a State agent gives rise to an envisaged future risk of harm sufficient to engage the *non-refoulement* rule, it would appear that relatively extensive procedural obligations materialise requiring that the risk to be assessed and determined in accordance with due process standards. In the migrant boat example, this would suggest that access to such facilities must be provided, whether on the intercepting boat or by disembarkation at a territory where such procedures are available. From the human rights perspective, the exercise of State authority over a person brings with it certain inescapable human rights obligations.

Conclusions: intersections between human rights and refugee law

This brief analysis of extraterritoriality shows that State obligations under international human rights law do not stop at its borders nor are they blind to events beyond them. Rather, the jurisprudence requires a State to take account of the human rights implications of expelling or removing an alien across such borders and to comply with human rights obligations when it exercises jurisdiction beyond those borders. Both requirements are concerned with extraterritoriality but from different standpoints and thus they apply different rationales.

Whereas refugee law pioneered the development of the *non-refoulement* principle, it is largely silent on whether this principle and other refugee law obligations apply when States act beyond their own borders. Indeed, this ambivalence is amply demonstrated in one of the few such cases to be decided on a refugee law basis before the courts: in a 1993 decision in *Sale*, the United States (US) Supreme Court held by a majority that refugee law treaty obligations did not apply when the US interdicted boats from Haiti on the high seas. Although the decision is much criticised, still it stands against the lack of any international tribunal for refugee law where its rationale might be challenged.

By contrast, recent jurisprudential developments in international human rights law strongly suggest that a State acting outside its own territory remains bound by the human rights version of the *non-refoulement* principle. However, of perhaps greater significance than the mere applicability of this principle of extraterritoriality are the far-reaching procedural implications that this entails, particularly in light of the recent jurisprudential advances in the human rights field confirming the existence of robust due process standards in cases where *non-refoulement* may be in issue. In brief, it would seem that the provision of access to proper procedures for making such determination is obligatory.

These findings are significant not only in their own right but also for how they bolster refugee law. Thus, in some human rights systems, the relevant procedural standards also require that refugee status be determined in accordance with the same due process guarantees. In other words, at least for people outside their country and in the hands of a State acting extraterritorially, the duty to determine human rights *refoulement* risk marches hand-in-hand with a requirement to determine refugee status. Alternatively, access to protection against *refoulement* on human rights grounds can serve as a backstop to refugee status, given the degree of overlap between the two.

Bibliography

Instruments

American Convention on Human Rights, 1969

Convention Against Torture, 1984

European Convention on Human Rights, 1950

International Covenant on Civil and Political Rights, 1966

Cases

European Court of Human Rights, 1989, *Soering v. UK*

European Court of Human Rights, 2012, *Othman (Abu Qatada) v. UK*

European Court of Human Rights, 2014, *Öcalan v. Turkey*

European Court of Human Rights, 2011, *Al-Skeini and Others v. UK*

European Court of Human Rights, 2012, *Hirsi Jamaa and Others v. Italy*

Human Rights Committee, 1994, *Chitat Ng v. Canada*

Inter-American Court of Human Rights, 2014, *Advisory Opinion OC-21/14 on Rights and Guarantees of Children in the Context of Migration and/or in Need of International Protection*

Commentaries

Cantor, D. J. (2014) 'Laws of unintended consequence? nationality, allegiance and the removal of refugees during wartime', in D. J. Cantor and J. F. Durieux (eds.), *Refuge from Inhumanity? War Refugees and International Humanitarian Law* (Leiden: Martinus Nijhoff), chapter 14.

— (2015) 'Reframing relationships: revisiting the procedural standards for refugee status determination in light of recent human rights treaty body jurisprudence', *Refugee Survey Quarterly* 34 (1), pp. 79–106.

Moreno-Lax, V. (2012) 'Hirsi v. Italy or the Strasbourg court versus extraterritorial migration control?', *Human Rights Law Review* 12 (3), pp. 574–98.

Noll, G.,(2005) 'Seeking asylum at embassies: a right to entry under international law?', *International Journal of Refugee Law* 17 (3), pp. 542–73.

Wilde, R. (2013) 'The extraterritorial application of international human rights law on civil and political rights', in N. Rodley and S. Sheeran (eds.), *Routledge Handbook on Human Rights* (London: Routledge), chapter 35.

17

Rethinking Muslim women's equal rights: faith, property and empowerment[1]

M. Siraj Sait

The pursuit of gender equality and women's empowerment, especially in parts of the Arab and Muslim world, struggles in the face of several conundrums. How can women's civil and political rights be strengthened without corresponding attention to their socio-economic rights and poverty alleviation? How could women's participation in the public sphere be expanded when their private and intra-household leverage remains limited? How could Muslim women's rights be sustainable through secular discourse in traditional and religious communities? How can innovative formulations of women's rights be transformed into workable tools and embedded in formal systems for practical gains for Muslim women in complex environments? Recent developments and efforts in the arena of women's access to resources and property offer some fresh approaches to women's empowerment.

Among the estimated billion Muslim women across the world, the index of rights and empowerment dramatically varies reflecting the diverse political, economic, legal and religious systems and contexts. The interconnectedness and indivisibility between individual freedoms and economic development has been long asserted and established, for example, by Amartya Sen linking individual capabilities and economic opportunities (Sen 1999) and is apparent among Muslim communities. Most civil and political rights dimensions, from the choice of hijab (veil or head dress), to the right to drive, to exercise of sexual and reproductive rights, or the ability to be leaders, underpin socio-economic rights dimensions. Striking among the issues is the often-limited access to property, inheritance and land for Muslim women. Yet, it is acknowledged that property and land are vital not only for women's livelihoods, housing and economic opportunity but such rights also enhance their physical security from

1 This research is a part of research funded by the Global Land Tool Network, UN-Habitat.

violence, consolidates their control over their own resources and choices, and encourages their public participation.

The obstacles that Muslim women generally encounter in acquiring property and land are invariably similar to other patriarchal and hierarchical societies, but several distinctive aspects of tradition and Islamic law often intervene. On the positive side, Islamic law, including the holy *Qur'an*, proposes an extensive range of personal property rights for Muslim women that includes the rights to acquire, hold, use and dispose of property and land freely in her own name (Sait and Lim 2006, 134). Historical evidence points to Muslim women being propertied well before their Western counterparts (Moors 1996; Shatzmiller 1995). Yet, Muslim women often inherit only half the proportion of shares as their equally placed male relatives, though in some circumstances they inherit equally or more. Numerous economic and religious explanations abound for this gender discrimination, primarily that women have no economic responsibilities toward their family, which is the exclusive male role. However, unmarried women, women-headed households, as well as wives increasingly working shatter the myth of the exclusive male breadwinner with positive implications for gender equality in Muslim communities and innovative approaches to inheritance within the traditional framework.

In contrast to other areas of legal reform in the Muslim world, the gender differentiated Islamic inheritance rules have mostly endured. Most Muslim women abstain from challenging the apparent discrimination as the detailed fixed rules are derived from the verses of holy *Qur'an* (about 35 verses). Islamic inheritance is still widely practiced and a 'pride' of the community given the famous dictum attributed to the Prophet to, 'equal one half the sum total of human knowledge!' (Makdisi 1994). David Powers, however, rightly points out that rather than static automatic division of shares, Islamic inheritance is a broader and dynamic system of multi-stage negotiations and planning rather than just a body of technical rigid rules (Powers 1993, 13). A series of estate planning strategies as well as post inheritance negotiations and adjustments take place. Indonesia provides an example of parallel and simultaneous inheritance processes with the formal demarcation through Islamic inheritance accompanying a more need-based and equitable allocation in accordance with tradition (*adat*), which is lodged with the local land office.

While Muslim women are often only entitled to half the male share, there is nothing in Islamic law that prevents women from having equal property and rights. Muslim women frequently argue that inheritance should be viewed holistically through interlinked intra-family and intergenerational property flow systems, which compensate their inheritance deficit. There are no gender restrictions on women receiving property or land under the *wasiya* (will) that is permissible up to a third of an estate. Women can, and often do, receive *hiba* (gifts) from family and outsiders at various stages in their life including marriage and beyond. There are other arrangements such as *waqf* (family endowments), which can theoretically be entirely for females. Associated with marriage are several payments including the *mahr,* which is payable by the bridegroom to the bride, payments as per the marriage contract, additional compensation for household work (*iwad*) maintenance during marriage and, in most countries, on divorce (*nafaqa*). In Iran, for example, women are entitled to wages for housework (*ojrat-ol mesal*). Islamic land laws also create gender-neutral opportunities to acquire land rights through 'enlivening' unused land productively (*mewat*) or preemption (*shufa*). However, formal mechanisms to compensate women for their deficient inheritance rights are yet to be developed.

Inheriting Muslim women face two broad challenges. First, women mostly inherit cash, jewels or movable property while immovable property flows away from women generally. This reflects the global female land ownership estimated at around merely 3 per cent. In many countries, land is constructed to be a male domain and women further are considered as members of their husband's family who would take property away from the family. Fragmentation of land due to widespread inheritance thereby impacting on viability and economic efficiency of land parcels also targets women (Sait and Tempra 2014). Thus, ensuring that women have choice over what they inherit is equally important. Second, women often 'voluntarily renounce' (*tanazul*) their inheritance rights in 'exchange' for other property or to preserve family relationships with more powerful family members and retain access to the family home. This custom is the focus of legal reforms, for example, in Jordan and Palestine, where renunciation is to be registered with witnesses and takes effect only after a period. An interesting spin-off argument is that if women can renounce their inheritance shares in favour of male relatives, nothing prohibits the reverse to ensure gendered equal property rights.

While inheritance for Muslim women has received considerable attention, the denial of marital property to women in most Muslim countries has not. While Islamic law is admittedly strong on women's personal property and guarantees inheritance, it is silent on a Muslim wife's claim to her share of marital property – that which is acquired during marriage. For Muslim women without adequate savings, uncertain inheritance, swift divorces, inadequate dower (*mahr*) and limited maintenance (*nafaqa*), denial of their share in marital property renders them effectively destitute or reliant on natal family or the State. Without an independent stake in marital assets, she retains no property rights acquired or accessed or ownership interest in their marital home or land (Safwat 1995, 6).

Under a UN-Habitat funded project, research has explored the Islamic legal framework of marriage and property to demonstrate that Islamic law in itself does not inhibit equitable, if not equal, marital property distribution among spouses (Sait 2013a). More persuasively, in over a dozen countries where Muslims reside as majority (or in multi-religious countries), community property regimes or sharing of marital property is far more widespread among

Muslims than assumed. The case studies of politically, geographically and jurisprudentially diverse Turkey, Kazakhstan, Indonesia, Malaysia, Morocco, Tunisia, Iran, Maldives, Tanzania, Kenya and South Africa underscore the complex but often accommodative relationship between marital property doctrines and Islamic principles. Furthermore, they offer opportunities for comparative legal reform in other countries.

Women's access to land is frustrated by the notion of the male as the head of the family. Hence property is legally registered in his name even if the woman has contributed directly or indirectly to the acquisition of the property. The traditional notion of the male as the head of the family has to be challenged. The University of East London produced provocative research showing that matrilineal kinship cultures (through the female line) and bi-lineal (through male or female) in Muslim communities are extensive (Sait 2013b). Dozens of case studies from various parts of the globe including India, Sri Lanka, Indonesia, Malaysia, Vietnam, Cambodia and Thailand, Algeria, Sudan, Burkina Faso, Ghana, Senegal, Kenya, Tanzania, Comoros, Mozambique and Malawi debunked the idea that Muslim women cannot be co-owners of property, if not head of the family. This is reflected in successful joint titling (where the names of male and females are registered) in several Muslim countries, including Indonesia. Encouragingly, several Muslim countries are moving away from the legal concept of the male as the head of the family; for example, the Mouduwana family code in Morocco (Aixelà Cabré 2007).

Several themes emerge from the analysis. Muslim marital property regimes are negotiated not merely from religious conceptions, but through its intersection with custom, family, kinship and the construction of property itself. In Muslim societies, legal pluralism prompts choices over marital property regimes between remnants of colonial law, modern constitutional and human rights provisions and Islamic, customary and secular laws. The varied legal reform methodologies of Muslim matrimonial property regimes include secularisation, Islamic re-interpretation, cohabitation of custom and Islamic law, and legal pluralism. Advocacy, research and legal reform recast Muslim women's rights but can remain paper aspirations that fail to materialise. Women are unable to assert their rights in the face of opaque or corrupt land registration systems or skewed land policies. Moreover, in their generalised form, women's property rights fail to support poor women on the specifics on how to access and retain land in the face of multiple challengers including land mafia, unscrupulous developers, official evictors or family competitors.

The Global Land Tool Network (GLTN) uses a tool-based approach to promote human rights and land security by developing tools that identify steps in interventions or mechanisms to deliver the objectives of human rights, outputs and outcomes. Through a multi-stakeholder process pro-poor, gendered and affordable tools are developed that indicate who does what where or when, providing information on substance, process and dispute resolution.

For example, in relation to access to marital property, several tools are required, such as registration of marriage and marriage contract as well as enabling responsive institutions dealing with marriage and divorce. Remarkably, GLTN has adopted an 'Islamic Mechanism' whereby the Islamic dimension needs to be considered and used positively where applicable.

Land and property rights are not simply about ownership documents with female names. They encompass individual, collective and customary rights to access, use and manage property within a continuum of rights framework. Straddling civil and political as well as socio-economic rights, they potentially strengthen autonomy, offset vulnerabilities, increase choices, improve access to credit and economic opportunities and facilitate equal participation in all walks of life. In view of their significance, property rights are a complex and contested arena. Muslim property regimes are negotiated through intersection of custom, religion, family, kinship and the construction of property itself. Thus, the battles for Muslim women's equal rights are not merely fought on the streets, podiums and protest lines but also inside the homes, through religious interpretation and negotiations with all stakeholders. Drawing on comparative interdisciplinary studies and rights-based approaches within Muslim discourses, the endeavour to develop authentic, context-specific tools continues afresh.

Bibliography

Aixelà Cabré, Y. (2007) 'The Mudawwana and Koranic law from a gender perspective: the substantial changes in the Moroccan family code of 2004', *Language and Intercultural Communication* 7 (2), pp. 133–43.

Makdisi, J. (1984) 'Fixed shares in intestate distribution: a comparative analysis of Islamic and American Law', *Brigham Young University Law Review* Rev. 267 (3), pp. 267–304.

Moors, A. (1996) *Women, Property and Islam: Palestinian Experiences -1920–1990* (Cambridge: Cambridge University Press).

Powers, D. S. (1993) 'Islamic inheritance system: a socio-historical approach', *Arab Law Quarterly* 8 (1), pp 13–29.

Safwat, S. M. (1995) 'What happens to the matrimonial home on divorce in Islamic law', *International Legal Practice* 20, pp. 1–12.

Sait, S. (2013a) 'Marital property in Muslim communities: Islamic law, custom and reforms', *Recht van de Islam* 27, pp. 33–53.

— (2013b) 'Women's property rights in Muslim matrilineal communities' *Journal of Islamic State Practices in International Law* 9 (1), pp. 1–35.

Sait, S. and H. Lim (2006) *Land, Law and Islam: Property and Human rights in the Muslim World* (London: UN-Habitat/ Zed Books).

Sait, S. and O. Tempra (2014) *Land Fragmentation in Muslim Communities: Traditional Challenges and Innovative Consolidation Approaches* (Washington DC: World Bank).

Sen, A. (1999) *Development as Freedom* (New York: Knopf).

Shatzmiller, M. (1995) 'Women and property rights in Al-Andalus and the Maghrib: social patterns and legal discourse', *Islamic Law and Society* 2 (3), pp. 219–57.

18

Power of the law, power to the people: pursuing innovative legal strategies in human rights advocacy

Tanja Venisnik[1]

The use of legal tools and mechanisms in human rights advocacy can play a significant role in the advancement of human rights. Although often difficult, complex and time-consuming, using legal strategies, particularly strategic litigation, in campaigning and advocacy can influence decision-making processes and bring actual changes in legislation, policy and practice. It can also help raise public awareness about a particular human rights issue and empower communities to claim their rights by involving them in designing and implementing legal advocacy strategies.

However, pursuing legal strategies to advance human rights is easier in some jurisdictions than in others. In countries where political space for human rights advocacy is limited and the rule of law weak, relying on human rights norms tends to be inefficient and can even prove counter-productive. In these cases, invoking other legal norms, such as environmental protection laws, can prove more useful for the improvement of the human rights situation on the ground.

Struggles of communities affected by large-scale development projects

In this respect, working on human rights issues in South East Asia (SEA) presents a particular challenge. There is a lack of openness to human rights discourse, and the implementation of human rights norms is weak, even if those norms are in fact a part of domestic law.[2] The inexistence of an effective

---

1   The views expressed by the author in this chapter are her own and are not necessarily endorsed by the organisation for which she works.

2   Most SEA countries have ratified core human rights treaties, such as the International Covenant on Civil and Political Rights (ICCPR) and the International Covenant on Economic, Social and Cultural Rights (ICESCR). However, none of the SEA countries have ratified the optional protocols establishing and providing access to complaints mechanisms under these two treaties. The only exception is the

regional human rights mechanism amplifies these challenges.[3] In these contexts where the judiciary lacks independence and is painstakingly inefficient, access to justice for human rights and environmental violations is often difficult.

Another element that poses further obstacles to the realisation of human rights in the SEA region is poorly regulated cross-border investment. As ASEAN is developing its Post-2015 agenda and moving towards regional economic integration, cross-border investments in the region will continue to intensify, especially investments from more developed countries in Asia towards less developed. These investments can bring numerous benefits to host countries, however, experience shows that large-scale development projects, such as hydropower dams, mines, agricultural plantations and coal power plants, bring significant risks to the environment and human rights, especially when implemented in countries with unstable economies and weak legal regimes, most notably in Lower Mekong countries such as Cambodia, Laos and Myanmar.

The pattern of dispossession is staggeringly clear: in the name of economic development, local communities who mostly rely on fishing and small-scale farming for their livelihoods face loss of land and other natural resources, degradation of the environment, loss of livelihoods and impoverishment. They see no or very little economic benefits for themselves and are forced to leave their homes and traditional livelihoods behind, further worsening their economic situation. Environmental degradation caused by such development projects, such as CO_2 emissions and water pollution, and the depletion of natural resources provoke displacement and violent conflict and can have negative implications, both direct and indirect, for the effective enjoyment of human rights.[4] Despite these recognised threats, many development projects in SEA are going ahead without enough attention to their environmental impacts (local as well as transboundary) and mitigation measures, prior community consultations or transparency and corporate accountability. As the frameworks for understanding and establishing extra-territorial obligations of states and corporate entities have only recently started to develop, communities lack legal remedies and avenues to express their concerns and have their grievances heard and addressed.

Philippines that ratified the first Optional Protocol to the ICCPR.

3   The member states of the Association of Southeast Asian Nations (ASEAN) adopted the Human Rights Declaration and established the ASEAN Intergovernmental Commission on Human Rights (AICHR), however, the Declaration is weak and not legally binding, whereas the AICHR remains a toothless body with no mandate to receive and investigate individual human rights complaints.

4   UN Human Rights Council, *Analytical study on the relationship between human rights and the environment, Report of the United Nations High Commissioner for Human Rights*, UN Doc. H/HRC/19/34 (16 December 2011).

Addressing environmental concerns plays an important role in addressing human rights issues and obtaining remedies for negative human rights impacts of environmentally unsustainable development projects. Despite notoriously weak implementation of laws in the Mekong region, lawyers, activists and communities are increasingly using environmental protection laws in order to support broader human rights advocacy efforts. For example, environmental impact assessment laws have been used to demand public participation in decision-making processes around development projects, whereas land laws have been invoked to address land grabs and protect indigenous peoples' rights.

In pursuit of meaningful remedies

However, seeking remedies in countries where violations occur is often simply not feasible nor effective due to lack of legal mechanisms, weak government-controlled judiciary and prominent vested interests, leaving project affected communities with no meaningful remedy.

In recent years, communities, activists and lawyers in the Mekong region have increasingly been using innovative legal strategies. They have been able to successfully turn to national human rights institutions (NHRIs) to seek redress for human rights abuses stemming from large development projects posing threats to local people and their environment. This especially relates to transboundary cases, such as the well documented Koh Kong Sugar Plantation Case in Cambodia. In 2006, hundreds of villagers in Sre Ambel district had their lands illegally confiscated and were evicted to make way for a large sugar plantation, operated by politically-connected Cambodian companies and controlled by Thailand-based Khon Kaen Sugar Ltd. (KSL).[5] Unable to obtain remedies in Cambodia, local communities filed a complaint to the National Human Rights Commission of Thailand (NHRCT) against KSL. In its recent final report in the case, the NHRCT invoked the UN *Guiding Principles on Business and Human Rights* and found that KSL was responsible for human rights violations against the affected communities through the business operations of its Cambodian subsidiaries and that the land grab was in violation of the right to life, the right to self-determination, including the right to manage and benefit from natural resources, and the right to development. Although NHRCT cannot issue binding decisions and can only make recommendations, its findings are nevertheless important for the overall campaign[6] and can also

5   KSL had an exclusive sales contract with Tate & Lyle Sugars (T&L) in the United Kingdom.

6   Koh Kong case is part of a global Clean Sugar Campaign that developed in response to rampant land grabs in Cambodia and serious human rights abuses and environmental damage caused by the Cambodian sugar industry. For more information about the campaign and the case, see Inclusive Development International, *Cambodia Clean Sugar Campaign*, available at http://www.inclusivedevelopment.net/sugar/

be used to support community claims in their litigation against T&L in the United Kingdom.[7]

Another example comes from Malaysia. In 2014, Cambodian and Thai communities filed a complaint to the Malaysian Human Rights Commission (SUHAKAM) against a Malaysian project developer, Mega First Corporation Berhad, building a hydropower dam in Laos (Earth Rights International 2014). Due to lack of political space and democratic institutions and legal mechanisms to address the issue in Laos the affected communities turned to a Malaysian institution. The communities claimed that if built, this dam, would very likely cause irreversible harm to regional fisheries in the Lower Mekong Basin, seriously affecting the lives, livelihoods and health of millions of people in Laos, Cambodia, Thailand and Vietnam. Yet the project developer did not study the transboundary impacts of the project or provide sufficient information about its impacts. It also failed to provide a meaningful opportunity to affected communities in Laos, Cambodia, Vietnam and Thailand to have their voices heard and to express their concerns about the project.

SUHAKAM initially accepted the complaint and conducted separate hearings with Mega First but ultimately concluded that it had no mandate to address a transboundary issue and therefore could not proceed further with the inquiry. It did, however, make recommendations to the Malaysian government to develop policies to monitor Malaysian companies operating abroad in order to ensure compliance with international human rights standards and adhere to the OECD *Guidelines for Multinational Enterprises* and establish a National Contact Point (NCP) complaints mechanism.

SUHAKAM's inability to conduct an inquiry into a transboundary case highlights legal difficulties of pursuing transboundary legal cases and the need to strengthen NHRIs and create an independent and functional regional human rights mechanism with a strong mandate. Despite the outcome, solely

---

(accessed 8 Oct. 2015); and Earth Rights International, *Case Study: Koh Kong Sugar*, available at http://www.earthrights.org/multimedia/video/case-study-koh-kong-sugar (accessed 8 Oct. 2015).

7   In 2013, the affected community filed a law suit in UK courts seeking compensation from T&L, arguing that under Cambodian law, the land and produce belonged to the Cambodian community and that T&L wrongly took the sugar cane and so must compensate the community for the stolen sugar. By following the money, the affected community was also able to use the Organisation for Economic Cooperation and Development's (OECD) Guidelines complaint mechanism and file a case with the US National Contact Point (NCP) against American Sugar Refineries (ASR), as owner of T&L, for its purchase of all of the sugar from the Koh Kong economic land concession. ASR withdrew from the mediation proceedings following the filing of litigation against T&L. Nevertheless, the US NCP called ASR to conduct a corporate human rights policy review process, a statement which was useful for other advocacy and campaigning efforts.

by filing the complaint as part of a broader campaign against this particular project as well as against the planned cascade of eleven Mekong mainstream dams, the communities were able to raise awareness about the environmental and human rights issues of the project and harness international support for their plight.

Unfortunately, even positive decisions by quasi-judicial bodies or even legally binding judicial decisions do not necessarily translate into the implementation of human rights due to the absence of enforcement mechanisms. National and international judicial and quasi-judicial bodies can render numerous landmark decisions against states, upholding international or regional human rights standards. However, if they are not enforced by states due to economic reasons and capital pressures, human rights violations cannot be properly addressed and remedied. One example comes from a region that has put in place a regional human rights body that can issue binding legal decisions. In its landmark 2010 decision in the case of the *Endorois indigenous community v. Kenya*, the African Commission on Human and Peoples' Rights (ACHPR) set a critical precedent that indigenous populations in Africa are legally entitled to collective ownership of their ancestral lands. Despite intensive lobbying from the Endorois community and NGOs and recent positive developments reflected in the creation of a government task force charged with addressing restitution of the lands to the Endorois, compensation for losses due to their eviction, and a benefit-sharing agreement, the implementation has been slow and more has to be done to achieve full and direct implementation of the ruling (Minority Rights Group International 2010; 2014).

These difficulties with enforcement highlight that relying solely on the law or litigation is evidently not enough but it can help lead to positive results, if combined with other advocacy strategies and pressure tools.

Law as a tool for building people's power

As with any advocacy efforts, lawyers and advocates, especially Western organisations operating in developing countries, should be very careful to make sure that they truly represent the 'asks' of the community and that they do not employ strategies that *they* think will benefit them. Obtaining the affected community's support and informed consent, based on consultation and community input, is crucial. To that end, victims of human rights and environmental abuses need to be educated about their legal rights and legal and advocacy options that they can use to advance their demands. Engagement with affected communities is indispensable for designing as well implementing legal advocacy strategies, making sure that they are the ones driving the process and linking legal strategies with grassroots campaigning.

The pursuit of legal strategies in human rights advocacy is more than filing lawsuits, complaints and petitions. It is first and foremost raising awareness of legal rights and building capacity of communities to understand decision-making processes, legal frameworks and legal avenues they can pursue to seek redress and protects their rights. Working closely with the affected communities on a legal case can lead to community empowerment as the process brings together the power of the law and the power of the people and provides an opportunity to create people's movements. Legal advocacy and strategic litigation efforts play into larger campaigning actions. Their ultimate aim lies beyond winning a particular legal case; it is about building people's power and helping create more equitable societies.

Bibliography

EarthRights International (2014) *No Fish, No Food: NGO Coalition Files Complaint Against Don Sahong Dam Developer* (20 October 2014), available at http://www.earthrights.org/media/no-fish-no-food-ngo-coalition-files-complaint-against-don-sahong-dam-developer (accessed 8 Oct. 2015).

EarthRights International, n.d. *Case Study: Koh Kong Sugar*, available at http://www.earthrights.org/multimedia/video/case-study-koh-kong-sugar (accessed 8 Oct. 2015).

Inclusive Development International, *Cambodia Clean Sugar Campaign*, available at http://www.inclusivedevelopment.net/sugar/ (accessed 8 Oct. 2015).

Minority Rights Group International (2014) *Kenyan Task Force formed to implement the 2010 Endorois ruling*, Press Release (29 September 2014), available at http://minorityrights.org/2014/09/29/kenyan-task-force-formed-to-implement-the-2010–endorois-ruling/ (accessed 8 Oct. 2015).

Minority Rights Group International (2010) *Landmark decision rules Kenya's removal of indigenous people from ancestral land illegal*, Press Release (4 February 2010), available at http://minorityrights.org/2010/02/04/landmark-decision-rules-kenyas-removal-of-indigenous-people-from-ancestral-land-illegal/ (accessed 8 Oct. 2015).

UN Human Rights Council (2011) *Analytical study on the relationship between human rights and the environment*, Report of the United Nations High Commissioner for Human Rights, UN Doc. H/HRC/19/34 (16 Dec. 2011).

19

Domestic incorporation of the United Nations Convention on the Rights of Persons with Disabilities in the Marshall Islands

Divine Waiti

The United Nations Convention on the Rights of Persons with Disabilities ('Convention') and its Optional Protocol were adopted on 13 December 2006, and were opened for signature on 30 March 2007.[1] It was described as 'the highest number of signatories in history to a UN Convention on its opening day'.[2] Unfortunately, this was less inclusive of the Asia-Pacific countries: the region was considered to have the lowest rate of signatures and ratification of the Convention (UNESCAP 2015). Only three countries in the Pacific (Australia, New Zealand and Vanuatu) have signed the convention at the time it was opened for signature, while most of the Pacific Islands countries became a state party some years later. The Republic of the Marshall Islands ('Marshall Islands') is the most recent Pacific island state to become a party to the Convention on 17 March 2015.

This paper gives an account of the domestic incorporation of the Convention on the Rights of Persons with Disabilities in the Marshall Islands. It is a personal reflection with some critiques and comments on some of the work involved in the process of translation of the Convention into domestic law. It first looks at the accession to the international convention; second, it reviews the formulation of policy which drives legislative measures and social policies; third, it discusses the legislative review and compliance process to fine-tune the national legislative framework; and fourth, it describes the adoption of a comprehensive non-discriminatory law in compliance with the Convention.

---

1   United Nations Enable (2015), *Convention on the Rights of Persons with Disabilities,* available at http://www.un.org/disabilities/default.asp?id=150 (accessed 11 Sept. 2015).

2   Ibid.

Accession to the Convention

While signing gives a state the expression of its intention to implement a convention, ratification legally binds a state to implement the convention. Where a state is unable to sign and ratify before the entering into force of the convention, accession would be the next process. For instance, the Republic of the Marshall Islands expressed its consent to be bound by the Convention by depositing its instrument of accession with the Secretary-General of the United Nations in New York after the coming into force of the Convention on 3 May 2008.

The ratification of human rights treaties has been an issue for Pacific Island countries for many years. Recently, the Marshall Islands, during its second Universal Periodic Review, was recommended to implement a number of core human rights treaties.[3] While some considered it lack of prioritisation for implementation, others said it is a matter of resources allocation to which most Pacific Islands countries are not prepared to obligate (Thomas 2009, 6). The Pacific Island countries, especially the small island developing states like the Marshall Islands, have common features of remoteness, smallness in size and capacities, limited resources, aid dependency and vulnerability to climate change and global economic shocks, and clearly resources allocation is the dominant factor.

Another feasibility factor also for the Marshall Islands is the lack of early interventions to engage both the government and civil society, especially for persons with disabilities, to rally support for ratification. It was in early 2013 a person was designated to the relevant government ministry to develop and implement a national disability inclusive policy for the Marshall Islands.[4] In 2014, a Disabled Peoples Organization (DPO) was established to empower persons with a disability to contribute to the development and the implementation of a disability strategy, policy and legislation. Following the establishment of the DPO, various consultations on the national policy on disability inclusion were undertaken. In a nutshell, there was clearly a lack of resources and capacity to build, educate and lobby leaders to ratify the Convention at the very early stage of the Convention. It should therefore be

3   (i)International Covenant on Civil and Political Rights and its Optional Protocols; (ii) the International Covenant on Economic, Social and Cultural Rights and its Optional Protocol; (iii) the Convention on the Elimination of all forms of Racial Discrimination; (iv) the Convention against Torture and its Optional Protocol; (v) the Convention on the Rights of Migrant Workers; (vi) the Convention for the Protection of All Persons from Enforced Disappearance; and (vii) the Convention on the Prevention and Punishment of the Crime of Genocide. UN Human Rights Council (2015), *Report of the Working Group on the Universal Periodic Review; the Marshall Islands,* UN Doc. A/HRC/30/13 (20 July 2015).

4   Republic of the Marshall Islands National Policy on Disability Inclusive Development 2014 – 2018, 9.

noted that considerable efforts must be taken by donor partners to collaborate and engage early, and must mandate inclusive developments to ratify human rights treaties.[5]

Formulation of national policy

Article 4 of the Convention affirms that a Government must protect and promote the rights of persons with disabilities in all policies and programmes. The Marshall Islands National Policy on Disability Inclusive Development was developed in 2014. It sets out a twin-track approach of a long-term vision for improving the well-being of those persons with disability, which includes the development of legislation and the building of capacity of persons with disability, and to promote activities that are inclusive for persons with disabilities in areas of employment, education, and health services and other social development. The policy was developed with the technical assistance of the United Nations Economic and Social Commission for Asia and the Pacific (UNESCAP)'s Pacific Office, the Pacific Islands Forum Secretariat and Pacific Disability Forum (PDF). Through this technical assistance, research and various consultations with a range of stakeholders, including persons with disabilities, were undertaken.[6]

Because the policy was formulated prior to the acceding to the Convention, much of the attention was drawn towards social policies and lobbying and supporting the government to accede to the Convention and less focus was on the legislative measures and approaches taken for domestic implementation. More specifically for the present purpose, an ideal policy must have a clear legislative framework that lays out the legislative measures needed for translation into law. It must be strongly supported and endorsed by the government and the relevant stakeholders. Furthermore, taking ownership and initiatives to implement a legislative policy agenda is very critical. In the Marshall Islands, the treaty domestication process was often prolonged due to lack of ownership and initiatives to drive successful implementation.

The social policy frameworks for inclusiveness of persons with disabilities must be clearly outlined as well. The policy must take a 'critical collaboration' approach (Wilkinson 2009, 18); where collaborative efforts must be 'between

---

5   A similar delay was faced with the ratification and implementation of the UN Convention Against Corruption until the UNDP Sub-regional Office was mandated to support the Pacific Island countries with their ratification process by engaging relevant stakeholders in various consultations and trainings. It was after a workshop was conducted for the Members of the Parliaments, that there was an overwhelming support to ratify the Convention and domesticate it into national laws.

6   Republic of the Marshall Islands National Policy on Disability Inclusive Development 2014–18, 9.

government and civil society and engages people with disability.' This is especially important in the Pacific where traditional languages, cultural beliefs and practices are usually not in conformity with the exercise of the rights of persons with disabilities (ibid., 18). Moreover, the social policy must have a broad-based framework (ibid., 19). Generally, in the Pacific, including the Marshall Islands, the social policy is always confined within the terms of education, health, employment, housing, or welfare without linkages on how each of these impact on the other. The Republic of the Marshall Islands must move away from the charity approach of treating persons with disabilities to a rights-based policy.

Legislative review and compliance

By acceding to the Convention, the Marshall Islands commits itself to enact domestic laws by adopting measures to improve the rights of persons with disabilities and to abolish legislation, customs and practices that discriminate against persons with disabilities. To ensure that these laws are in conformity with the Convention, a comprehensive legislative and compliance review is required. At the time the policy was formulated, a legislative review of the existing laws of the Marshall Islands was carried out by the Pacific Islands Forum Secretariat prior to the ratification of the Convention. Like other Pacific Island countries, the Marshall Islands lacked a comprehensive legislation that adopts disability rights measures in conformity with the Convention. This includes the Constitution of the Marshall Islands, which guarantees fundamental rights and freedoms that equally apply to all persons, including persons with disabilities. Only a few pieces of legislation identified provided for specific targeted issues, especially for the social areas of health, education, transport, family and other social policy matters; for instance, a specific provision in the Motor Traffic Act provides for reserved parking space for persons with disabilities.

The legislative compliance review identified several issues that needed addressing. First, the lack of comprehensive non-discriminatory legislation for persons with disabilities that leads to the development of relevant legislation to promote, protect and enforce the rights of persons with disabilities. Second, the little piece-meal legislation identified mainly focused on social protection and benefit provisions in education and employment, and health services for mental illnesses. This is where a paradigm shift is called for in attitudes and approaches to persons with disabilities. The focus and approach should shift to recognise persons with disabilities having and enjoying the same human rights just like any other person. Persons with disabilities should no longer be considered 'objects' of charity in need of social protection but are 'subjects' with rights, who are capable of claiming those rights and making decisions for their lives based on their free and informed consent as well as being active members of society.[7] Third, the existing legislation lacks disability friendly terminology. While the Convention emphasises the harmonisation of disability friendly terminology, the common references to persons with disabilities in the laws of the Marshall Islands are 'insane', 'handicap', 'disability', 'physical disability', 'mental disability', 'person suffering from mental disorder', 'mental retardation', 'mental deficiency', 'mental impairment', 'mentally or physically incompetent', 'incompetent', 'mental incapacity', 'mentally incapacitated', 'physically helpless', 'mentally defective' and 'disabled person'.[8] Article 1 of the Convention defines 'persons with disabilities' to 'include those who have long-term physical, mental, intellectual or sensory impairments which in interaction with various barriers may hinder their full and effective participation in society on an equal basis with others'. Such changes to legislative language must go hand in hand with public awareness and training on disability neutral language and references. Language used in legislation must be used at administrative and practical levels.[9]

The next step in the legislative review is to seek constitutional amendments and consequential amendments to the existing legislation that is not in conformity with the provisions of the Convention. These processes are forthcoming during the writing of this chapter.

Adopting a comprehensive legislation

While the type of legislation each country should adopt depends on the existing laws and the particular legal system of a State party,[10] the Marshall Islands opted to adopt a comprehensive legislation that covers the general provisions of rights of persons with disabilities in Article 3 of the Convention and other specific provisions of the Convention. The *Rights of Persons with Disabilities (RPD) Act 2015 ('Act')* was introduced to the Parliament (*Nitijela*) and passed its first reading. It was assigned to a Standing Committee on Judiciary and Government Relations for public consultations. The committee reported its findings to the parliament and the bill was voted on and unanimously adopted on 28 September 2015.

---

7   The traditional Marshallese approach has been one of caring for disabled family members who are regarded as weak; protecting them from harm and from the possibility of being teased, bullied or mocked. This is at odds with the current approach, which aims to empower persons with disabilities.

8   CRPD Legislative Review (2014), Government of the Marshall Islands with the Assistance of the Pacific Islands Forum Secretariat, 16.

9   Ibid.

10 The legal system of the Marshall Islands is largely influenced by the US legal system, having been a US Trusteeship from 1945 until its independence in 1986, and currently being in free association with the US under the 2004 Compact of Free Association with the US. The country has a unicameral parliamentary system where the Parliamentarians are vested with powers to enact, repeal, revoke or amend any law in force in the Republic.

The two main purposes stated in the *Act* are (i) to declare, protect, promote, fulfill and enforce the rights and freedoms of persons with disabilities on an equal basis with others; and (ii) to implement the legal obligations of the Marshall Islands as a State Party to the Convention.[11] In implementing the legal obligations, the *Act* adopted the principles contained in Article 3 of the Convention, in relation to persons with disabilities, which are:

    a. respect for the inherent dignity, individual autonomy including the freedom to make one's own choices, and independence of persons;

    b. non-discrimination;

    c. full and effective participation and inclusion in society;

    d. respect for difference and acceptance of persons with disabilities as part of human diversity and humanity;

    e. equality of opportunity;

    f. accessibility;

    g. equality between men and women;

    h. respect for the evolving capacities of children with disabilities and their right to preserve their identities including the respect for the dignity and value of older persons with disabilities, and respect for the inclusive community-based features of Marshallese culture.

Most of these principles listed above underpin the interpretation of substantive provisions that are outlined in the *Act*. The *Act* also elaborates on the recognition given to persons with disabilities to participate fully in all aspects of life including the recognition of equal treatment, protection and benefit of the law, the recognition for active participation in all decision making processes, policies and programs, including those that directly concern them, and recognition of the right to voice their concerns including on: approaches to implementing development; implementation, monitoring and reviewing of policies; legislation; and services to ensure that they effectively meet their requirements.[12]

One of the cornerstones to any legislation on the rights of persons with disabilities is 'reasonable accommodation'. The Convention stipulates that a failure to afford a person reasonable accommodation amounts to discrimination on the basis of disability (UN-DESA et al. 2007, 60). In adopting this provision of the Convention, Section 2 of the *Act* defines as follows:

In this Act:

    a. "reasonable accommodation" means appropriate modifications and adjustments, whether of a rule, a practice, an environment, a requirement or otherwise, in order to ensure the full participation by persons with disabilities in an activity, on an equal basis with others;

---

11 Section 3(2) of the *Rights of Persons with Disabilities (RPD) Act 2015*.

12 Section 3(3) of the *Rights of Persons with Disabilities (RPD) Act 2015*.

    b.   the nature and limits of the duty to accommodate must be determined on a case by case basis and include factors such as the accommodation required, the size of the entity involved, and the resources available; and

    c.   the duty must be reasonable and must not impose a disproportionate or undue burden.

These provisions take account of the principle that 'if the accommodation required would impose a disproportionate or undue burden on the person or entity expected to provide it, then a failure to do so would not constitute discrimination' (ibid., 60). The proposed legislation for the Marshall Islands sets out the factors that should be taken into account when assessing the reasonable accommodation.

In conclusion, one could deduce from these discussions that the domestication of the Convention is an on-going process for the Pacific Island countries. So far, most of the Pacific Island countries have signed and ratified or have acceded to the Convention. The Marshall Islands, as the most recent in the Pacific to become a State party, has taken a step further (as has Australia and New Zealand), to domesticate its national laws in conformity with the Convention. While some differences may exist in the legal systems of the other Pacific Island countries, the pioneering of this piece of legislation and the involvements in the domestic process in the domestication of the laws for the Marshall Islands, would offer some lessons for other Pacific Island countries. It is highly recommended that domestication of the national laws relating to the rights of persons with disabilities be accomplished for rest of the Pacific Island countries.

Bibliography

Republic of the Marshall Islands National Policy on Disability Inclusive Development 2014–2018.

Thomas, P. (2009) 'Introduction: disability, disadvantage and development', *Development Bulletin* 73, pp. 5–9.

United Nations Department of Economic and Social Affairs (UN-DESA) (2007), Office of the United Nations High Commissioner for Human Rights, Inter-Parliamentary Union, 'From Exclusion to Reality: Realizing the Rights of Persons with Disabilities', in *Handbook for Parliamentarians on the Convention on the Rights of Person with Disabilities and its Optional Protocol* (Geneva: United Nations).

United Nations Economic and Social Commission for Asia and the Pacific (UNESCAP) (2015), *Disability: Challenges and Opportunities*, available at website http://www.unescap.org/our-work/social-development/disability/about. (accessed 11 Sept. 2015).

United Nations Enable (2015) *Convention on the Rights of Persons with Disabilities*, available at http://www.un.org/disabilities/default.asp?id=150 (accessed 11 Sept. 2015).

United Nations Human Rights Council (2015) *Report of the Working Group on the Universal Periodic Review; the Marshall Islands*, UN Doc. A/HRC/30/13 (20 July 2015).

Wilkinson, A. (2009) 'Making disability policy in the Pacific rights-based policy', *Development Bulletin* 73, pp. 18–21.

20

The Inter-American Human Rights System: notable achievements and enduring challenges

Par Engstrom

In the teaching, as well as in the historiography, of international human rights, regional human rights systems, with the partial exception of the European Court of Human Rights, remain marginalised. This is regrettable for a number of reasons; not least because the richness of regional experiences with human rights offers us a more nuanced understanding of the enduring attraction of human rights around the world (as well as a better sense of the diversity and contentious political struggles that characterise them), than that prevailing in the current literature proclaiming the endtimes of human rights (Hopgood 2013; Moyn 2012).

Nowhere can this be seen better than in the region of the Americas, where the Inter-American Human Rights System (IAHRS) emerged to play a vanguard role in the development of the modern international human rights regime. This short piece briefly reviews the current state of the IAHRS, and highlights its key achievements, as well as some of the many challenges it faces. It should be pointed out, from the outset, that any list of achievements and challenges inevitably depends on perspective, the specific yardstick adopted, and, in particular, the understanding of what could be reasonably expected from the IAHRS.

Achievements

In the interest of brevity, five points serve to illustrate how the IAHRS has emerged as the central human rights reference point in the region of Latin America, in particular.

First, in terms of rule-making, both the Inter-American Commission on Human Rights and the Inter-American Court of Human Rights perform a crucial function in the development of human rights standards. The Court has developed progressive human rights jurisprudence through its rulings. The Commission also serves an important function in this regard through its thematic reports and development of policy guidelines, for example, in such diverse areas as freedom of expression, rights of detainees, and land rights. The IAHRS has become increasingly ambitious not only in terms of the types of human rights challenges it deals with, but also in terms of what it demands from states. In particular, the Inter-American Court's evolving policies of reparations now span from monetary compensation to victims, symbolic reparations (e.g. memorials), to demands for state reforms and criminal prosecutions of individual perpetrators.

Second, another important function of the IAHRS concerns monitoring and evaluation of state practices. From its institutional origins as a 'classical' intergovernmental regime, the IAHRS has evolved into an institutionally robust and autonomous system. Its legal and institutional architecture is today dramatically different from the one originally set up in the immediate period following the adoption of the American Declaration of the Rights and Duties of Man in 1948. An independent court and commission are invested with the mandate to respond to individual claims by judging whether domestic legislation, policies and particular actions or omissions violate international state commitments.

Third, the IAHRS has established itself as an important advocacy actor in its own right. The Commission, in particular, has developed a fairly comprehensive set of tools in addition to individual cases that range from public diplomacy in the form of press releases, public hearings, onsite visits, interim measures (precautionary mechanisms), to behind the scenes negotiations with state officials and individual petitioners. The IAHRS also performs a significant indirect advocacy role by providing an important platform for human rights NGOs, some of which have been very adept at integrating the IAHRS into their advocacy strategies in order to bring pressure for change in their domestic political and legal systems.

Fourth, the IAHRS performs important accountability functions; though we should not exaggerate their relative robustness. Various mechanisms have been developed by the IAHRS to hold states accountable for human rights violations: Court rulings, compliance reports, etc. True, these are weak accountability mechanisms in the sense that there are no enforcement mechanisms in place to hold states responsible for implementation. For example, there is no clearly mandated political compliance mechanism, as assumed by the Committee of Ministers in the European system. Still, accountability can operate through various channels, including primarily domestic accountability mechanisms – e.g. in the form of mobilisation of public opinion around specific cases, raising awareness through media strategies, and domestic litigation processes.

Finally, the focus on domestic politics highlights the ways in which the IAHRS has become increasingly inserted into domestic policy and legislative debates on specific human rights issues across the region. This signals a gradual move away from a dominant focus on contentious litigation of individual cases to attempts to settle cases through friendly settlement procedures. This 'change of paradigm' in human rights activism also reflects the increasing use of individual cases to promote broader government policy changes and institutional changes.

Challenges

The achievements of the IAHRS are considerable when considered against the often inhospitable regional conditions prevailing throughout the Americas. Yet, these institutional successes contain the seeds of the many challenges facing the IAHRS. Two particularly important challenges stand out, concerning accessibility and 'impact', on the one hand, and the politically contested status of the system, on the other.

First, does the system 'matter' to those mostly in need, however conceived? This is, in part, a question of access and participation. Individuals and groups in the Americas may submit complaints of human rights violations to the Inter-American Commission, and the Commission may refer cases to the Inter-American Court if the country involved has accepted the Court's jurisdiction. Indeed, individual access to the human rights regime has strengthened over time as the system has evolved into a judicial regime with a procedural focus on the force of legal argumentation and the generation of regional human rights jurisprudence. The system institutionally legitimises and discursively encourages civil society participation, and it formally empowers citizens to bring suit to challenge the domestic activities of their own government. No longer, therefore, a mere quasi-judicial entity with an ill-defined mandate to promote respect for human rights in the region, today's IAHRS offers important opportunities for human rights activists to bring pressure for change in their domestic political systems.

We should not, however, overstate the general accessibility of the IAHRS to individual petitioners. The capacity of actors to access and to mobilise the IAHRS is highly unequal. Successfully accessing the IAHRS requires a high level of legal and technical expertise. In practice, this means that the vast majority of petitions that actually gain traction in the system – i.e. proceed beyond initial submission phase – are advocated by NGOs. Nonetheless, engaging in the process of litigation before the IAHRS involves very lengthy proceedings that imply a significant drain on already limited resources for NGOs that pursue litigation. The process before the System is also highly unpredictable and partial state compliance with IAHRS decisions is often the best outcome petitioners can realistically hope for. Still, the Commission receives an increasing number of petitions, which has led to a significantly increased case-load, and back-log of cases, for the system.

Another aspect to note in this regard is that individuals and groups do not have direct access to the Court. The Commission only has the mandate to bring cases to the Court. In practice, this means that Commission lawyers have been delegated the responsibility to act on behalf of individual petitioners. This also often means that professional human rights NGOs bring cases representing individual victims or group of victims. The structure of these dynamics is such that potential problems of representation and legitimacy may arise, with NGOs pursuing interests and objectives that are not necessarily aligned with the needs and interests of individual victims; e.g. devising litigation strategies that may that seek to leverage individual cases to bring about broader policy and legislative changes.

Even more crucial, however, is the limited capacity of the IAHRS. The system is able to process only a small number of the petitions submitted. Given the vast human rights challenges facing contemporary societies in the region, moreover, only a miniscule proportion of the violations committed on a daily basis are presented to the IAHRS. This reality raises, once again, several thorny yet important questions concerning the accessibility of the system, particularly for marginalised and vulnerable individuals and groups in the region, who, arguably, are those most in need of the system's support for the realisation of their human rights.

A second challenge to the system concerns its future, in light of political changes in the region, as well as broader global shifts that may increasingly challenge the international human rights regime. The IAHRS is subject to some very significant legitimacy and authority challenges. From the perspective of the users of the IAHRS, as already highlighted, the system can appear fairly inaccessible. The internal functioning of the system also raises questions concerning its perceived legitimacy and efficacy. For example, one common criticism is that the Commission is not transparent in its selection of what cases to accept. The length of proceedings also undermines claims that justice is rendered even in cases that result in a Court ruling. Doubts are regularly raised concerning the competence, independence, and motivations of individual members of the Commission and the Court.

Moreover, there is significant regional variation with regards to the formal adherence to the system. This is reflected in the uneven adoption of regional human rights instruments by OAS member states. Indeed, one of the contentious issues surrounding the IAHRS is precisely its uneven ratification record. While most Latin American states demonstrate a high degree of formal commitment to the IAHRS, the US, Canada, and most of the English-speaking Caribbean have not ratified the American Convention on Human Rights (1969) and have not accepted the jurisdiction of the Court. In addition, states are regularly questioning the authority of the System; some are withdrawing their diplomatic and financial support. Trinidad and Tobago's withdrawal from the American Convention following its continuing commitment to the death penalty took effect in 1999; Venezuela announced its withdrawal in 2012, and the Constitutional Court of the Dominican Republic ruled in 2014 to withdraw from the Inter-American Court's jurisdiction (Engstrom 2015). This raises the problem of having one system seeking to apply general principles of law in a regional context characterised by considerable heterogeneity between, and within, countries.

Indeed, the significant political tensions surrounding the IAHRS in recent years highlight that processes of institutional development are not necessarily progressive, nor unidirectional. True, there may be a basic recognition of certain fundamental human rights principles in the Americas. Beyond this basic normative consensus, however important it may be, recent debates within the OAS concerning the scope and direction of IAHRS reforms suggest that some states question the institutional direction of travel of the IAHRS. Trenchant criticisms in recent years from several member states may suggest that the IAHRS is on the verge of overstretching its institutional mandate. Efforts by states to constrain or rein in the IAHRS may need to be seen, moreover, in the broader context of an uncertain future for the global human rights regime in light of the wider implications of shifting global power balances from which the Americas as a region is not immune. As power shifts globally, as well as regionally in the Americas, competing understandings of sovereignty that emphasise sovereign equality may reassert themselves challenging the demands and expectations of human rights advocates. Indeed, debates within the OAS in the context of the recent IAHRS reform process reflect an enduring and deep disquiet towards external monitoring and sanction of the human rights record of governments. From this perspective, it may be argued that it is precisely the institutional development of the IAHRS, in ways that have escaped the control of states, which has prompted significant pushback by certain groups of states within the OAS.

Without doubt, it is important to recognise the very real limitations of the IAHRS and to be sober about the many challenges the system is facing. Yet, there continue to be reasons to be cautiously optimistic about the future of the IAHRS. Despite its institutional weaknesses, the IAHRS performs many important functions as outlined above. As reflected in steadily increasing petitions to the Commission, the system continues to be turned to by those who have been denied justice at home. The demand from victims and their relatives, and human rights organisations across the region, remains, in other words, robust and growing.

Bibliography

Engstrom, P. (2015) 'El Sistema Interamericano de Derechos Humanos y las Relaciones Estados-Unidos América Latina' *Foro Internacional*, LV(2), pp. 454–502.

Hopgood, S. (2013) *The Endtimes of Human Rights* (Ithaca, NY: Cornell University Press).

Moyn, S. (2012) *The Last Utopia: Human Rights in History* (Cambridge: Harvard University Press).

Notes on contributors

Olivia Ball was a psychologist working with refugees in her hometown of Melbourne prior to completing the MA in Understanding and Securing Human Rights in 2002. She also worked as a teaching assistant on the programme in 2002. During her MA student placement at the Medical Foundation for the Care of Victims of Torture, she wrote *Every Morning, Just like Coffee: Torture in Cameroon* (2002), a report described by Africanist Milton Krieger as 'crucial on the Cameroon human rights front'. In 2006, she co-authored *The No-Nonsense Guide to Human Rights* (New Internationalist Publications 2006) with Institute of Commonwealth Studies then senior lecturer Paul Gready, which was described by the *Law Institute Journal* as 'by far the best condensed summation of the modern human rights movement anywhere'. In 2013, she completed a PhD in human rights at Monash Law School and in 2014 she co-founded Remedy Australia.

José-Manuel Barreto graduated from the MA in Understanding and Securing Human Rights in 2000. He is currently based at the Max Planck Institute for European Legal History, Frankfurt. Most recently he was a fellow at the Käte Hamburger Center for Advanced Study in the Humanities 'Law as Culture', University of Bonn. He works on the epistemological decolonisation of human rights and international law, and explores their history and theory in the context of modern imperialism. His research also addresses questions about art, the 'turn to emotions' and the human rights culture, and about how to defend human rights telling stories. He edited *Human Rights from a Third World Perspective: Critique, History and International Law* (Cambridge Scholars Publishing 2013). He has been a visiting lecturer at the Universidad de los Andes in Bogota, and a Postdoctoral Research Fellow at Goldsmiths, University of London and at the Humboldt University of Berlin. He has also eight years of experience as a human rights lawyer in Colombia. He studied philosophy and law at the National University and the Externado University of Colombia, respectively. After finishing the MA at the Institute of Commonwealth Studies, he obtained a PhD in law from Birkbeck, University of London.

Bridget Burrows is currently ActionAid international campaigner on tax justice. ActionAid's Tax Power campaign is working in 20 countries across the world. ActionAid is part of the Global Alliance for Tax Justice. Bridget previously worked at Amnesty International as the Africa Regional Campaigner on Slums, working with residents of informal settlements in six African countries to defend their housing rights, and specialises in international social and economic justice campaigning. She worked in Nairobi, Kenya for five years, and graduated with an MA in Understanding and Securing Human Rights in 2003, with a dissertation on economic and social rights in Uganda.

David James Cantor is director and founder of the Refugee Law Initiative and a reader in human rights law at the Institute of Commonwealth Studies, School of Advanced Study, University of London. He is an Economic and Social Research Council (ESRC) Future Research Leader and editor-in-chief of the International Refugee Law book series published by Martinus Nijhoff. David worked as a Legal Officer for the Refugee Legal Centre and also with UN High Commissioner for Refugees (UNHCR). He has undertaken extensive fieldwork in Colombia, where his work has influenced law and policy, as well as in other countries in the Andean region, Central America, Southern Cone and Mexico. He has trained governments from across the globe, participated in UNHCR expert meetings and runs a new distance-learning MA in Refugee Protection and Forced Migration Studies at the University of London.

Sumi Dhanarajan is an international development practitioner specialising in the impacts of the private sector upon poverty and human rights. Currently undertaking a PhD in law at the National University of Singapore (NUS), she has previously served as a researcher at the Centre on Asia and Globalisation at the Lee Kuan Yew School of Public Policy at NUS, senior policy advisor on the private sector at Oxfam GB, a senior legal advisor to the Hong Kong Democratic Party's Secretariat for Legislative Councillors and as Human Rights Officer to the Malaysian Bar Council. She is a Trustee of the Business and Human Rights Resource Centre. Sumi holds an LLB from Durham University, an MA in Understanding and Securing Human Rights from the Institute of Commonwealth Studies (1997/98) and an LLM from the National University of Singapore. She was called to the Bar in 1998.

Par Engstrom is lecturer in human rights at the Institute of the Americas, University College London. He worked previously at the Human Rights Consortium (HRC) at the School of Advanced Study, University of London, from the creation of the HRC in 2009 until 2012, where he also taught on the MA in Understanding and Securing Human Rights. He is currently leading a major research project on the impact of the Inter-American Human Rights System. His other research interests include torture prevention, transitional justice, and the International Relations of the Americas. Prior to entering academia he worked at the Office of the High Commissioner for Human Rights (OHCHR) in Geneva, Switzerland.

Paul Gready is the director of the Centre for Applied Human Rights, University of York, and co-editor of the *Journal of Human Rights Practice*. Prior to moving to York he convened the MA in Understanding and Securing Human Rights at the Institute of Commonwealth Studies, University of London. His research interests include transitional justice, development and human rights, and culture/the arts and human rights. Paul is currently lead researcher on two multi-year grants: 'Transformative Justice in Egypt and Tunisia' (ESRC); and the 'Transitional Justice Barometer in Tunisia' (NWO).

Farid Hamdan started his career with Amnesty International in Palestine from 1995 to 2002. After obtaining his MA in Understanding and Securing Human Rights in 2002–3, he worked with the Palestine Central Election Commission as a Coordinator for one of the election districts from 2003–4. He later moved to work as a Civil Society Specialist at Care International, West Bank & Gaza. In 2005, he worked as a Legal Coordinator and Outreach Specialist in ARKAN for a Rule of Law Project between Chemonics International and Massar Associates. In 2006, he joined the UN mission in Sudan as a human rights officer and served in the Darfur region. In 2010, he joined the Office of the High Commissioner for Human Rights (OHCHR) Regional Training Centre in Qatar and is currently leading the Technical Cooperation Project for Saudi Arabia.

Sally Holt is a senior research fellow at the University of East London's Centre on Human Rights in Conflict specialising in minority rights and the inclusion of vulnerable and marginalised groups. Her recent research and publications have focused on the management of cultural diversity and conflict prevention and on the participation of women in conflict-affected contexts. From 2000–4 she was legal officer at the office of the OSCE High Commissioner on National Minorities (HCNM) and was contracted in 2010 as consultant in developing the HCNM *Ljubljana Guidelines on Integration of Diverse Societies*. As an adviser to the Initiative on Quiet Diplomacy (2008–12) she oversaw the development of a 'toolkit' of conflict prevention resources for policy-makers and practitioners. She has also managed a research programme for the Aga Khan Foundation (UK) on the social inclusion of Muslim populations in Europe (2007–8), and carried out policy-oriented research on peacebuilding and security challenges at Bradford University (2004–7). She regularly undertakes consultancies for NGOs and IGOs including the UN, European Commission and OSCE. She was awarded her MA in Understanding and Securing Human Rights (with distinction) in 1998.

Catherine Klirodotakou graduated from the MA in Understanding and Securing Human Rights in 2006 and has worked in the field of human rights and international development since. Her specific areas of expertise are in securing women's human rights and gender equality in sub-Saharan Africa and

Latin America. Currently she works at Womankind Worldwide, supporting programmes and partnerships with women's rights organisations in Sierra Leone, Liberia, Peru and Bolivia, to help build a strong and vibrant women's movement and deliver gender transformative programming in women, peace and security, reducing violence against women and increasing women's civil and political participation. She is also a trustee and treasurer of the UK Gender and Development Network. Prior to Womankind, Catherine worked at ChildHope UK and in education.

Corinne Lennox is senior lecturer in human rights in the Institute of Commonwealth Studies and associate director of the Human Rights Consortium at the School of Advanced Study, University of London. Her research focuses on issues of minority and indigenous rights protection, civil society mobilisation for human rights and on human rights and development. She has worked for many years as a human rights practitioner with various NGOs, including at Minority Rights Group International, and has been a consultant on minority rights for the UNDP, the UN Office of the High Commissioner for Human Rights and the UN Special Rapporteur on Minority Issues. She is co-editor of the *Handbook of Indigenous Peoples' Rights* (Routledge 2015) and co-editor of *Human Rights, Sexual Orientation, and Gender Identity in the Commonwealth: Struggles for Decriminalisation and Change* (Institute of Commonwealth Studies/Human Rights Consortium 2013).

James Manor established the MA in Understanding and Securing Human Rights when he was director of the Institute of Commonwealth Studies during the mid-1990s. He has also taught at Yale, Harvard and Leicester Universities and at the Institute of Development Studies, Sussex. He is now Emeka Anyaoku professor emeritus in the Institute of Commonwealth Studies where he coordinates a major international research programme on recently intensified efforts to tackle poverty and inequality in Brazil, India, China and South Africa.

Gaia Marcus graduated from the MA in Understanding and Securing Human Rights in 2010. She manages Centrepoint's Youth Homelessness Databank, which aims to provide the youth homelessness sector with sustainable ways of measuring its scale, impact and outcomes. In her previous role as senior researcher at the Royal Society for Arts (RSA), Gaia led research for the Connected Communities programme and the organisation's social network analysis. Gaia's work examined the role of social networks in building resilient, empowered communities in promoting mental wellbeing and in building human capabilities in everything from education to social entrepreneurship. Gaia has experience with community-based practice and research ranging from the meaning of torture in Chile, to working on social innovation with the UnMonastery project in Matera, Italy, one of the world's oldest cities. She cycles for fun, and sings because she needs to.

Esther Ojulari is a PhD student within the interdisciplinary programme on human rights at the Institute of Commonwealth Studies, University of London. Her research is an analysis of the social construction of group rights for Afro-descendant people in Colombia. Esther has an MA in Understanding and Securing Human Rights (2010) in which she focused on Afro-descendant children's rights and an undergraduate degree in sociology focused on race, ethnicity and multiculturalism. Esther has worked previously for ChildHope UK and for several years as a consultant for the UN Office of the High Commissioner for Human Rights in the area of human rights for people of African descent.

M. Siraj Sait is professor of law and director of the Centre for Islamic Finance, Law and Communities at University of East London (UEL). A graduate of Universities of Madras and Harvard, he was a Chevening scholar at the Institute of Commonwealth Studies in 1997–9. He is a well-known human rights lawyer with a background as a government official and Human Rights Prosecutor in India. His development expertise includes land and housing policies, refugee and post-conflict studies, gender equality and rights in the Muslim world. An ex UN-Habitat official, he helped set up the Global Land Tool Network and has been consultant to UNHCR, UNICEF and FAO. His recent work includes drafting laws for Somalia, head of evaluation of UN projects in Iraq and the UN Advisory Group on Gender Issues. His research and impact study was highly rated in the UK Research Excellence Framework exercise 2014.

Smita Shah is a senior teaching fellow with the Centre for Access to Justice at University College London (UCL) Faculty of Laws. She is a barrister at the Bar of England and Wales and for over 10 years practised in the areas of family law, international human rights and international humanitarian law. Her specialism in practice was representing legally aided vulnerable clients in child protection and domestic violence cases. Her international work has a focus on child rights and women's rights; she has been an invited member of UNICEF UK research advisory board and undertaken child protection capacity building for UNICEF Nigeria. She has carried out rule of law projects in Palestine and Myanmar and undertaken workshops in Algeria and Turkey on women's rights. She is the co-founder of the Freedom of Expression Student Law Clinic. She graduated from the MA in Understanding and Securing Human Rights in 2001 and has an LLM in International and Comparative Law from Columbia University.

Damien Short is director of the Human Rights Consortium (HRC) and a reader in human rights at the Institute of Commonwealth Studies, School of Advanced Study. He has researched and published extensively in the areas of indigenous peoples' rights, genocide studies, reconciliation projects and environmental human rights. He is currently researching the human rights impacts of extreme energy processes (e.g Tar Sands and Fracking – see the designated HRC website http://extremeenergy.org). He is a regular academic contributor to the United Nation's 'Expert Mechanism on the Rights of Indigenous Peoples' and an academic consultant for the 'Ethical Trade Task Force' of the Soil Association. He is also assistant editor of the *International Journal of Human Rights* and convenor of the British Sociological Association's Sociology of Rights Study Group and an active member of the International Network of Genocide Scholars.

James Souter is a post-doctoral research fellow in the School of Politics and International Studies at the University of Leeds, where he is contributing to a project entitled 'The Responsibility to Protect in the Context of the Continuing "War on Terror": A Study of Liberal Interventionism and the Syrian Crisis', funded by Research Councils UK (grant number ES/L013355/1). Since graduating from the MA in Understanding and Securing Human Rights in 2009, James has interned and worked for the Immigration Advisory Service in London and Bristol, and completed an MSc and a DPhil at the Refugee Studies Centre, University of Oxford. He has published articles in *Political Studies*, the *Journal of Refugee Studies*, and (with Jason Ralph) *International Affairs*. James defended his thesis, entitled 'Asylum as Reparation', in 2014.

Laila Sumpton graduated from the MA in Understanding and Securing Human Rights in 2012, and currently divides her time between working as a youth engagement officer at international children's charity Plan UK and as a freelance poet. Laila is working on her first collection and regularly performs her poetry on human rights themes, with a particular focus on conflict and refugee rights. She co-edited the Human Rights Consortium's anthology *In Protest: 150 poems for Human Rights* (Human Rights Consortium 2013) and delivers poetry workshops at universities, schools, hospitals, museums and charities. She is a trustee of Bosnian youth arts NGO Most Mira along with fellow MA alumna Sue MacMillan and is a member of the Keats House Poets.

Tanja Venisnik is a qualified lawyer and human rights specialist with over 10 years of professional experience in both the private sector and the international public sector. Her career as a lawyer includes a rich variety of experiences, ranging from representing corporate clients in intellectual property cases to practicing EU law at the European Court of Justice in Luxembourg. After shifting her career towards human rights, Tanja became involved in human rights research, advocacy and training, focused on minority and indigenous peoples' rights. She conducted human rights training for Rakhine migrant students in Mae Sot, Thailand, and later moved to the Philippines to work as a Human Rights and Accountability Advisor for an NGO responding to the devastating effects of Typhoon Haiyan. Tanja currently works for EarthRights International as a Mekong legal coordinator, focusing on the development and implementation of legal strategies in human rights and environmental advocacy. She is especially interested in issues surrounding the right to information and public participation in connection to large-scale development projects. Tanja holds an MA in Understanding and Securing Human Rights (2013).

Divine Waiti is Legal Counsel for the Parliament of the Republic of the Marshall Islands. He graduated from the MA in Understanding and Securing Human Rights in 2005, where he was a Chevening Scholar from the Solomon Islands, the country of his birth. The Marshall Islands is a small island state located at the center of the Pacific Ocean between Hawaii and Australia. Since graduating from the MA, he has worked in various legal fields including in-house legal counsel for governments, as a public defender representing people in court, and now parliamentary counsel. In his role as the Parliamentary Counsel for the Marshall Islands, he has drafted laws relating to human rights, including the Convention on the Rights of the Child and the Convention on the Rights of Persons with Disabilities. He also responds to government consultations and parliamentary inquiries, undertaking drafting and review of policies and laws relating to the human rights treaties.

Human Rights Consortium

SCHOOL *of* ADVANCED STUDY
UNIVERSITY OF LONDON

MA in Understanding and Securing Human Rights

Feeling inspired to pursue post-graduate studies with us?

About the degree

The MA in Understanding and Securing Human Rights is the longest-running interdisciplinary, practice-orientated human rights MA in the UK. The degree aims to develop students as human rights practitioners and enable them to engage with the intellectual and philosophical foundations of human rights. The result is a degree which is:

- **Cutting-edge**, engaging with human rights debates and emergent issues at the forefront of scholarly research;
- **Policy-oriented**, seeking to enable students to examine human rights issues from a practical, solution-oriented perspective as well as a scholarly one;
- **Career-orientated**, aiming to develop the next generation of human rights defenders, advocates and researchers through a special emphasis on building practical skills, including in campaigning, fundraising, and research.

Bursaries and grants

- The **James Manor Bursary Scheme** awards up to four bursaries per year, each equivalent to 50% of the applicable tuition fee. They are open to Home, EU and Overseas students.
- The **Routledge/Round Table Scholarship** is open to Overseas students from Commonwealth countries (outside of the UK). The award is worth £12,000. In addition, the awardee will receive a 50% fee waiver, enabling them to use the studentship for maintenance costs.
- The **Professor Dame Lillian Penson Memorial Trust** provides travel grants for students to support their studies.

Degree highlights

- Support for internships – We offer individually-tailored support in finding internships with human rights organisations in and around London, which will complement your studies and professional goals, and enable you to establish networks within the field.

- Annual Geneva study tour – We organise a one-week tour including visits to the United Nations and meetings with human rights advocates.
- Students also benefit from participating in the activities and events of the Human Rights Consortium, including attending its wide range of conferences and seminars, or getting involved in the Consortium's research projects.

Degree structure

The degree comprises three compulsory modules, three optional modules and a dissertation. Upon graduating, students will receive a degree awarded by the University of London.

Three modes of study are possible: 12 months full-time or part-time over 24 months or 36 months.

Further information:

www.sas.ac.uk/hrc/graduate-study

Student field trip to Geneva, 2013.

Lightning Source UK Ltd.
Milton Keynes UK
UKOW05f1110120317
296404UK00003B/147/P